CHURCHILL

Churchill examines the influential career of Winston Churchill, British Prime Minister during the Second World War and from 1951–1955. It analyses his career from his earliest appointments as Liberal President of the Board of Trade and Home Secretary to his premiership of the 1950s. Three chapters are dedicated to his controversial leadership of 1940–1945. The book examines a wide variety of sources including historiographical analyses, contemporary newspaper accounts and excerpts from Churchill's speeches.

Samantha Heywood is Head of Corporate Education Programmes at the Imperial War Museum. She previously taught History at the Cabinet War Rooms and Havant College.

QUESTIONS AND ANALYSIS IN HISTORY

Edited by Stephen J. Lee, Sean Lang and Jocelyn Hunt

Other titles in this series:

CHURCHILL

SAMANTHA HEYWOOD

ROUTLEDGE

London and New York

First published 2003
by Routledge
11 New Fetter Lane, London EC4P 4EE

Simultaneously published in the USA and Canada
by Routledge
29 West 35th Street, New York, NY 10001

Routledge is an imprint of the Taylor & Francis Group

Typeset in Akzidenz Grotesk and Perpetua by Keystroke,
Jacaranda Lodge, Wolverhampton
Printed and bound in Great Britain by TJ International Ltd,
Padstow, Cornwall

British Library Cataloguing in Publication Data
A catalogue record for this book is available from the British Library

Library of Congress Cataloging in Publication Data
Heywood, Samantha, 1966–
　　Churchill / Samantha Heywood.
　　　p. cm. – (Questions and analysis in history)
　　Includes bibliographical references and index.
　　　1. Churchill, Winston, Sir, 1874–1965. 2. Great Britain–Politics
and government–20th century. 3. Prime ministers–Great Britain–
Biography. 4. World War, 1939–1945–Great Britain. I. Title.
II. Series.
DA566.9.C5 H345 2003
941.084′092–dc21
[B]
　　　　　　　　　　　　　　　　　　　　　　　　　　2002031811

ISBN 0–415–28672–7 (hbk)
ISBN 0–415–23016–0 (pbk)

CONTENTS

ILLUSTRATIONS

SERIES PREFACE

Most history textbooks now aim to provide the student with interpretation, and many also cover the historiography of a topic. Some include a selection of sources.

So far, however, there have been few attempts to combine *all* the skills needed by the history student. Interpretation is usually found within an overall narrative framework and it is often difficult to separate the two for essay purposes. Where sources are included, there is rarely any guidance as to how to answer the questions on them.

The Questions and Analysis series is therefore based on the belief that another approach should be added to those which already exist. It has two main aims.

The first is to separate narrative from interpretation so that the latter is no longer diluted by the former. Most chapters start with a background narrative section containing essential information. This material is then used in a section focusing on analysis through a specific question. The main purpose of this is to help to tighten up essay technique.

The second aim is to provide a comprehensive range of sources for each of the issues covered. The questions are of the type which appear on examination papers, and some have worked answers to demonstrate the techniques required.

The chapters may be approached in different ways. The background narratives may be read first to provide an overall perspective, followed by the analyses and then the sources. The alternative method is to work through all the components of each chapter before going on to the next.

ACKNOWLEDGEMENTS

The author and the publishers would like to thank the following for permission to reproduce material:

Extract from *Churchill on the Home Front* by Paul Addison published by Jonathan Cape, used by permission of the Random House Group Limited. Cartoon by David Low: 'Winston's Persuasive Eloquence', originally published in the London *Evening Standard*, reprinted by permission of Atlantic Syndication. Extract from *Churchill and the Soviet Union* by David Carlton, reprinted by permission of Manchester University Press. Cartoon 'A Family Visit' reprinted by permission of Punch Limited. Extract from the First Report of the Dardanelles Commission (published as a series entitled 'Uncovered Editions'), reprinted by permission of Tim Coates, Publisher of Archives. Extract from speech made by Churchill on 18 June 1940, reprinted by permission of Churchill Archives Centre, Churchill Papers, CHAR 9/140A/55. Photograph of Churchill on the steps of No. 10, May 1940, the official war photographs 'The Prime Minister's tour' and 'A Frenchman lights a famous cigar' and the poster 'Let us go forward together', reprinted by permission of the Imperial War Museum.

While every effort has been made to trace and acknowledge ownership of copyright material used in this volume, the publishers will be glad to make suitable arrangements with any copyright holders whom it has not been possible to contact.

CHRONOLOGY

Date	National/International	Churchill
1900	Von Bülow becomes German Chancellor	Made a daring escape from a Boer prison camp Enters Parliament as Conservative MP for Oldham
1901	Queen Victoria dies, succeeded by Edward VII	
1904		March: Churchill leaves Conservatives to join the Liberals
1905	December: landslide victory for Liberal Party in the general election	
1906	Moroccan Crisis	January: elected as MP for Manchester NW: appointed Under-Secretary of State for the Colonies
1908		Marries Clementine Hozier appointed President of the Board of Trade: Elected MP for Dundee
1909	People's Budget introduced	First daughter Diana born
1910	Edward VII dies, succeeded by George V Two general elections in	February: appointed Home Secretary

February and November
destroy Liberal majority in the
House
November: Tonypandy;
suffragette protests in
Westminster, 'Black Friday'

1911 January: Battle of Sidney Street   Son, Randolph, born
Parliament Act passed   October: appointed First Lord
General Strike threatened   of the Admiralty
July: Agadir Crisis

1913 Failure of negotiations for   Failed attempt to kidnap son
'naval holiday' with Germany: Randolph by suffragettes
bill to increase naval spending

1914 Outbreak of war   Daughter, Sarah, born

1915 February–December: Gallipoli   November: Churchill resigns
campaign
May: Coalition government
formed

1916 January: Last soldiers evacuate Churchill serves in France with
Gallipoli   the Scots Guards
July: Battle of the Somme
December: Lloyd George
becomes Prime Minister

1917 Russian Revolutions in   July: returns to government as
February and October   Minister of Munitions
March: publication of
Dardanelles Report

1918 November: Armistice   Appointed Secretary of State
December: Lloyd George's   for War and Air
coalition wins 'khaki election' Advocates British intervention
Allied intervention in Russian   in Russia
Civil War   Daughter, Marigold, born

1919 Treaty of Paris (Versailles   Visits Versailles conference
settlement)

1920   Appointed Secretary of State
for the Colonies
Youngest daughter, Marigold,
dies

1921		Participates in Anglo-Irish negotiations and guides the bill through Parliament
1922	Anglo-Irish Treaty passes Commons Chanak Crisis Fall of Lloyd George coalition	October: Churchill loses seat in Dundee; excluded from Parliament Last daughter, Mary, born
1923		Fails to win re-election as Liberal candidate for Leicester Publication of *The World Crisis*
1924	Conservative victory in the general election	Churchill stands for election as an independent candidate for Epping, and wins November: Baldwin appoints Churchill as Chancellor of the Exchequer
1925	Britain returns to the Gold Standard Coal dispute begins	
1926	Samuel Commission reports on the coal industry May: the General Strike	Churchill runs the government newspaper, *British Gazette*, during the General Strike
1928		Conflict with Neville Chamberlain over de-rating scheme
1929	Conservatives defeated in the general election Wall Street Crash October: Irwin Declaration on India	Churchill breaks with Conservative leadership over tariffs Loses a fortune in the Wall Street Crash
1930		January: resigns from the Business Committee of the Conservative Party
1931	Economic crisis leads to formation of a National Government September: Britain abandons the Gold Standard	December: knocked over by a taxi in New York and seriously injured

October: landslide victory for
National Government

1932   May: first speech warning of a
new war in Europe
Visits Germany in the summer
Seriously ill with paratyphoid in
autumn

1933 Hitler becomes Chancellor of   Speaks against defence cuts,
Germany   and critical of strength of RAF
Publication of *Marlborough*

1935 India Act passed   Appointed to the Air Defence
Research Committtee

1936 Abdication Crisis   March: passed over as Minister
March: Germany reoccupies   for the Coordination of Defence
the Rhineland   Supports Edward VIII in the
July: Spanish Civil War breaks   Abdication Crisis
out
November: Berlin–Rome Axis

1937 May: Neville Chamberlain   Supports policy of
becomes PM   non-intervention in Spanish
Civil War

1938 February: Eden resigns   Advocating alliance with France
March: Anschluss   and Russia against Germany
May: war scare over German   Churchill's speech criticising
threat to Czechoslovakia   Munich leads to attempts to
September: Munich   de-select him from his Epping
Conference   seat

1939 March: Germany occupies   September: Churchill
Bohemia and Moravia; Britain   appointed First Lord of the
guarantees Polish, Turkish   Admiralty and enters Cabinet
and Greek independence
April: conscription introduced
May: Pact of Steel between
Italy and Germany
August: Nazi–Soviet Pact
Anglo-Polish Treaty
September: Poland invaded by
Germany and the USSR

Britain and France declare war
on Germany

1940 April–May: Norway campaign
May: Nazi invasion of Belgium,
Netherlands, Luxembourg and
France. British retreat from
Dunkirk
June: French surrender
July–September: Battle of
Britain
September: first raids of the
Blitz

May: made Prime Minister and
forms National Government

1941 June: Nazi invasion of USSR
December: Pearl Harbor; US
entry into the war; British
surrender Hong Kong to Japan

August: signs the Atlantic
Charter with FDR at Placentia
Bay
December: Arcadia conference
in Washington

1942 February: fall of Singapore to
Japan
March: Japan occupies Burma
June: fall of Tobruk
October: British offensive in
North Africa; victory at El
Alamein
November: Torch Allied
landings in North Africa

June: second conference at
Washington
June: vote of confidence in
House of Commons
August: flies to Moscow to tell
Stalin there will be no second
front in 1942

1943 February: German surrender
at Stalingrad
May: Axis collapse in North
Africa
July: Allied invasion of Sicily
September: Allied invasion
of Italy
December: Teheran
conference

January: meeting with FDR at
Casablanca results in decision
to fight for the 'unconditional
surrender' of Germany and
Japan
August: Quebec conference
December: serious heart attack
and pneumonia

1944 January: Anzio landings at
Monte Cassino, Italy
June: D-Day landings at
Normandy
August: Allies liberate Paris;

October: meeting with Stalin
results in the 'percentages'
agreement on eastern and
central Europe

Warsaw uprising
September: Allies begin
liberation of Germany

1945 January: Soviet forces liberate
Warsaw
February: Yalta conference:
Dresden bombed
April: German surrender in Italy;
Hitler commits suicide: FDR
dies
July: Potsdam conference;
Labour victory in general
election
August: atomic bombs
dropped on Hiroshima and
Nagasaki; Japan surrenders

1946	February: crisis in Iran Truman Doctrine	March: Iron Curtain speech September: 'united states of Europe' speech at Zurich
1947	June: Marshall Plan for European Recovery	Exhibits his paintings at the Royal Academy for first time
1948	Berlin Blockade and Allied Airlift USSR detonates its first atomic bomb	
1949	April: NATO Treaty signed USA detonates first H Bomb	
1950	February: slim Labour victory in general election June: outbreak of Korean War	
1951	October: Conservative victory in general election	October: becomes Prime Minister
1953		October: awarded Nobel Prize for Literature
1954	Geneva Conference	
1955		April: resigns as Prime Minister

1

RADICAL, 1900–1911

BACKGROUND NARRATIVE

'I have mostly acted in politics as I felt I wanted to act.'[1]

The tone of Churchill's long parliamentary career was set by his maiden speech to the Commons in February 1901. Flouting tradition, he chose to make remarks about the Boer War, then in progress, which he knew to be controversial with his own party, the Conservatives. From the outset, then, he found it difficult to place loyalty to his party above loyalty to himself. Having been elected MP for Oldham in 1900, he quickly found himself opposing many of the Conservatives' policies: increased spending on the army, the post-war settlement with the Boers and, after 1903, Joseph Chamberlain's Tariff Reform campaign.

His vehement opposition to Tariff Reform was what drove Churchill to leave the Conservatives in March 1904. However, he joined the Liberal Party only after an attempt to form a 'centre party' had failed. This attraction to a political 'middle ground' is a recurring theme throughout his career, but it was out of reach this time. Instead, he found that he would have to join the opposition if he was to have a significant career in politics – and this he certainly meant to have. Often described as 'a young man in a hurry', his defection from a party that was losing its popularity with voters and its political unity to one which stood a good chance of forming the next government laid him open to accusations of opportunistic ambition.

Churchill was not an obvious Liberal. In particular, his previous hostility to the policy of Home Rule in Ireland, a policy central to the Liberal Party, had seemed to rule out his ever joining them. Yet join them he did. His undoubted talent as an orator and parliamentarian meant that after the Liberals' landslide victory in the 1906 election he was well placed to enter government in a junior post only five years after entering Parliament. His career with the last Liberal government of the century illustrates well how turbulent and troubled these years before 1914 were.

As Under-Secretary of State for the Colonies (1906–1908) Churchill was plunged into the surge of anxiety over Britain's fitness to cope with her imperial responsibilities, an anxiety inspired by her poor performance during the Boer War of 1899–1902. Arguing for restraint and reconciliation, Churchill was instrumental in the establishment of 'responsible government' in South Africa. In 1908 he was rewarded for his industry with a Cabinet post, President of the Board of Trade. Thrust into the arenas of social and working conditions, and of industrial relations, Churchill forged ahead with an ambitious programme of reform. Establishing labour exchanges to help the unemployed and drafting legislation to improve conditions for the 'sweated' trades and for miners made Churchill a highly visible public figure. Working in tandem with Lloyd George at the Treasury, he led a party revival. Together they became known as the 'heavenly twins' of New Liberalism.

ANALYSIS (1): HOW LIBERAL WERE CHURCHILL'S POLICIES IN THE YEARS 1908–1911?

This is a question of definitions. How far was Churchill a politician in the liberal tradition, which had dominated British politics throughout the nineteenth century, or how loyal was he to the doctrine and policies of the Liberal Party, of which he was such a prominent member during these years? And even within the broad base of that party were there policies or beliefs of Churchill's which did not fit, and which placed him at some distance from his political colleagues? Because Churchill defected not once but twice – from the Conservatives in 1904 and from the Liberals in 1924 – the issue of where his loyalties and political beliefs really lay was one that fascinated his contemporaries as much as it does historians today.

Churchill held many beliefs common to the liberal tradition; beliefs in individual freedom, in progress and in reform. He also believed in the goodness of humanity, writing in 1910 that 'it is natural to men ... to be virtuous and honest'.[2] From this flowed his commitment, while Home Secretary, to a programme of extensive prison reform. Had his tenure there not been overtaken by events it would have been the dominant feature of his work at the Home Office. His reforms were intended to make more humane the prison and punishment system. Thus his reduction of the period of solitary confinement into which all new prisoners were routinely put, from nine months to one; his instructions that the length and gravity of the sentence be appropriate to the crime committed; and his attempts to reduce the number of petty criminals, young offenders and debtors being imprisoned. He introduced lectures and libraries to prisons, to improve conditions not just for prisoners' bodies, but their minds.

Commitment to reform had been a distinguishing feature of the Liberal Party, in contrast to the Tories. And, of course, Churchill had begun his political life as a Tory, leaving it over a matter of political principle. Joseph Chamberlain's campaign for Tariff Reform of 1903 was abhorrent to Churchill, who organised the Free Food League in opposition to it. Free trade had been a central tenet of the Liberal Party since the repeal of the Corn Laws in 1846, as it had been of liberalism. Chamberlain's attempt to abandon this orthodoxy split the Tory Party and led to the ascendancy of the Liberals after their landslide victory at the polls in 1906. Having crossed the floor only two years earlier, Churchill stood to gain much from this victory. Some critics believed his joining the Liberal Party had had more to do with ambition than conviction, and indeed Churchill was rewarded with an office in the new government, as Under-Secretary of State for the Colonies.

In this position Churchill was able to implement a policy that the Liberal Party had only recently adopted. 'The keynote of Liberal imperial policy would be to replace the coercive attitudes of Unionism with conciliatory approaches appropriate to a party of progress and humanity.'[3] In his first post Churchill implemented the granting of responsible (or self-) government in the southern African states, establishing a model and precedent for settlements elsewhere that the Liberal Party believed was progressive and right. In this respect Churchill stood in the 'imperialist' faction of the party together with Asquith, as the party struggled to redefine its attitude towards governing an empire whose expansion under the Tories it had traditionally opposed. Having served in the army in various parts of the empire, Churchill was convinced that it was 'a great engine of civilisation and an instrument for good'.[4]

As the son of Lord Randolph, Churchill's position on the Irish problem was much more complex. His father had supported the Unionists of Ulster and coined the phrase 'Ulster will fight and Ulster will be right'. Initially, Churchill had supported this position, which made his conversion to the Liberal policy of Home Rule sensational. His visit to Belfast in 1912, to speak in support of Home Rule in a strongly Unionist region, nearly resulted in rioting and injury to him. Later, as First Lord of the Admiralty, he ordered that warships patrol the coast during the tensions following the Curragh 'mutiny' of 1914, to emphasise the government's intention that Home Rule be established, by force if necessary.

However, it is in the arena of social reform and improvement that Churchill built his reputation as one of the most important Liberal Party members of the day. In partnership with David Lloyd George, Churchill led a revival of the party's fortunes. The so-called 'People's Budget' of 1909 became the benchmark of this new approach. The budget required an increase in the taxation of the wealthy to fund a number of social reforms aimed at the poor. It was radical in the nature of the new taxes to be introduced, the amount of money to be raised, and because its explicit aim was to fund welfare projects for the sick, unemployed and widowed. As President of the Board of Trade Churchill's ministerial responsibilities were in these very areas and he supported the budget from its inception throughout its stormy passage through Parliament. He had already committed himself to the provision of pensions for certain categories of workers through the Old Age Pensions Act of 1908 and was busy with the second half of the National Insurance Act by which some workers would contribute to a fund for the sick and unemployed. Other legislation to improve working conditions included the bill for shop workers and the more successful Coal Mines Act of 1911. Churchill was particularly concerned by the cyclical nature of some jobs and determined to resolve this problem through the 1909 Trade Boards Act, by which a system of labour exchanges (where vacancies could be advertised to unemployed workers) was established. He went further, advocating the creation of a Committee of National Organisation in which a number of ministries would work together to fund and manage a programme of public works to employ workers during times of high unemployment.

Both this proposal and the People's Budget were radical solutions that made explicit use of state powers to create and fund a system of welfare provision. In advocating this, Churchill and Lloyd George contributed to the creation of the policies of their party. Faced with problems rooted in widespread poverty the two men abandoned the Gladstonian principles of low state intervention and low taxation, convinced that only radical solutions would do. Similarly, both of them were attracted to the notion of cross-party cooperation or government by coalition, so that these problems could be tackled without the distractions of party politics. 'New Liberalism' as practised by Churchill and Lloyd George, both dynamic, energetic and professional politicians, revived the party and gained (briefly) the support of working men. However, although their reforms provided the basis for a welfare state, neither man had intended to create such an institution. Churchill's commitment to social reform stopped well short of socialism, which he claimed, 'seeks to pull down wealth; [whereas] Liberalism seeks to raise up poverty'.[5] Churchill was a radical Liberal in that he aimed at fundamental changes and reforms to assure minimum standards of life and work, and he was not a revolutionary. His radicalism sometimes even led to him being accused of authoritarianism.

Paul Addison, historian of Churchill's domestic policies, has written that 'He embodied, to a remarkable extent, both the reforming and the conservative potential of the last Liberal Government'[6] and that 'His policies fully reflected the authoritarian strand in Edwardian social thought.'[7] Eugenics was one such strand, and greatly interested Churchill during his time as Home Secretary. His proposals for the sterilisation of the physically and mentally 'unfit' stemmed from a belief in the need for selective breeding to strengthen the British race. Unacceptable now as a respectable opinion, he was not alone in his attraction to eugenics then. Influential thinkers like Beatrice and Sidney Webb advocated the concentration of vagrants into penal camps, based on this system of thought. Churchill's support for sterilisation programmes for the 'unfit' stemmed also from his humanitarianism. He believed that sterilisation programmes were a humane solution for disabled people, enabling them to live in the community without 'fear' of passing on their disability to any offspring, and thus releasing them from the institutions in which most were otherwise forced to live.

Much more controversial at the time was Churchill's approach to the social and industrial unrest that appeared to dominate the years 1910–1911. Violet Bonham Carter was a close friend of Churchill's at this time and later wrote of him, 'he was never quite a Liberal. He never shared the reluctance which inhibits Liberals from invoking force to solve a problem.'[8] Indeed, his reaction to the protests of 1910 and 1911 betrayed his other face: 'He was prepared to countenance social reform, provided it was regulated and ordered by the government: he was not prepared to suffer dictates from below that threatened the social order he held dear.'[9] So, while prepared to extend the powers of the state to effect social reform, Churchill was not prepared to meet demands that came from the people. In his readiness to despatch troops to various parts of the country in response to the strikes that dominated this period, Churchill's authoritarianism was revealed. Churchill was 'identifiably different from many of his colleagues',[10] in his Tory, aristocratic and military background. Here, Pelling has written that 'his own reputation as a soldier was against him'[11] and that even when he was not to blame for the violence that characterised the industrial unrest of this time, he nevertheless was blamed. His apparent eagerness for confrontation frightened a number of his colleagues in government and ruined his relationship with organised labour for many years.

At base then, Churchill was bound by a belief in, and commitment to, the existing social order. Perhaps he was not so much a Liberal as a Tory Democrat. His father had invented the phrase Tory Democracy without really defining it. At the outset of his career in politics Churchill claimed, 'I am a Tory Democrat . . . I regard the improvement of the condition of the British people as the main end of modern government.'[12] Having declared that 'I think we should try to improve the lot of the masses of the people through the existing structure of society,'[13] it could be argued that this is just what Churchill set out to do. The fact that he did so through holding office in a Liberal government may have been irrelevant to him. Certainly, it was felt that as soon as he moved to the Admiralty in 1911 his previous commitment to social reform appeared to melt away, in favour of a militarism not part of Liberal tradition. Henceforward Churchill was never to show much interest in issues of social policy again.

In 'a career of absolute self absorption'[14] Churchill found little space for ideology of any kind, including religion, a fact which accounts in large part for the ease with which he was able to move from one political party to another, without requiring drastic adjustments to his political beliefs. While following in the broad liberal tradition of British politics, he found it both awkward and unnecessary to commit himself to any one set of party policies. Never a typical Tory or Liberal, he was, however, always a radical who attacked an issue with breathtaking energy and determination to bring about fundamental change and improvement.

Questions

1. Why did the 'People's Budget' of 1909 cause so much controversy?
2. Why did the 'new liberalism' fail to win the support of the working-class electorate?

ANALYSIS (2): WHY DID CHURCHILL ATTRACT CONTROVERSY SO FREQUENTLY WHILE HE WAS HOME SECRETARY?

'The progress of a democratic country is bound up with the maintenance of law and order.'[15] Written while he was at the Home Office, Churchill's words go a long way to explaining how he lost his reputation as one of the foremost social reformers of the Liberal Party. As Home Secretary he was responsible for the maintenance of public order 'and it was a responsibility which he discharged with great seriousness: as he did so at a time of social unrest, his naturally conservative instincts rose to the surface'.[16] This shift, from champion to villain of working-class interests, centred on events during November 1910 during which Churchill was engulfed by a blaze of critical publicity.

A wave of strikes and unrest in the coalmines of South Wales culminated on 8 November at Tonypandy with the accidental killing of a protestor. Earlier that day Churchill had reversed the local chief constable's request for troops, instead insisting that the local police be reinforced with police, not soldiers, from London. He had also made a public request to the striking miners to stop rioting in exchange for prompt and sympathetic attempts to settle their dispute. It was only when this attempt failed and the violent disturbances continued that Churchill decided after all to send in troops. Churchill was immediately criticised for having sent them in too hastily, causing bloodshed. In fact, by delaying their arrival he probably prevented more violence. Nevertheless, his reputation as someone determined to break strikes by force and at any cost was established by this episode. Perhaps the condemnation of Churchill was made all the more bitter by surprise and disappointment that someone who had been, at the Board of Trade, a champion of radical reforms for the benefit of the poor and unemployed had so easily resorted to force when faced with their protests.

The feeling that Churchill's response had been too belligerent was reinforced only days later, on 'Black Friday', 18 November 1910. During the six-hour-long struggle to control suffragette demonstrators outside the Houses of Parliament, the police used inappropriately physical tactics to remove and arrest the mostly female protestors. Once again Churchill, who as Home Secretary was directly responsible for the Metropolitan Police Force, found himself under virulent attack. With very little evidence, he was accused of having given special orders to the police deliberately to bully and humiliate the protestors. In fact, as Addison has pointed out, 'Churchill, who at once recognised that something discreditable had occurred, intervened to order the release of most of the women arrested.'[17] He did so again for the 185 women arrested a few days later during their demonstration in Downing Street. This leniency, together with Churchill's previous concessions to suffragette prisoners by granting them privileges as political prisoners, was given no credit. It was the accusations of brutality, and of incompetence in dealing with the protests, that stuck. As Home Secretary he shouldered the blame for his police force's heavy-handedness at a time when they and politicians alike were inexperienced and uncertain in the face of such unprecedented protest from women.

A third and peculiar episode just a few weeks later apparently provided yet more evidence of Churchill's bellicose interventionism. The 'Siege of Sidney Street' in January 1911 was a storm in a teacup, whisked up by anti-immigrant feelings at the time and by Churchill's curious behaviour. A small band of foreign criminals suspected of robbery, the murder of three policemen and of being anarchists had been cornered by police in a house in Sidney Street in the East End of London. Troops had been called and shots fired. Hearing of the siege, Churchill rushed to the scene in time to watch fire break out and burn the house to the ground, leaving the remains of two people inside. Later, the decision to allow the house to burn was attributed to Churchill and, whether true or not, even he admitted his attendance was unwise and that he had been impelled to go 'by a strong sense of curiosity which perhaps it would have been as well to keep in check'.[18] Subsequent newspaper coverage of the episode was sensational and Churchill's role severely criticised. Charmley has written, 'the episode seemed to epitomise Churchill's defects . . . egocentricity and boyish enthusiasm'[19] while Violet Bonham Carter has written that 'despite its relative triviality it is one of the most characteristic and revealing episodes of his life'.[20]

Of course, Churchill was distinguished from his fellow ministers by the very fact that he alone had a military – not an academic or professional – training. His confrontational style displayed a militaristic approach that was anathema to Liberals. The apparent ease with which he resorted to force became ever more evident throughout the summer of 1911, to the growing unease of his colleagues. This was a summer dominated by unprecedented industrial unrest, fears of economic and even social breakdown, mounting discontent in Ireland, the constitutional crisis and escalating tensions with Germany at Agadir. Strikes by seamen, dockers, transport and railway workers appeared to spread like wildfire from one city to another, so that the supply of basic foodstuffs appeared to be under threat. 'These trade unionists in their crazy fanaticism or diseased vanity are prepared to starve the whole population, including of course their own families and all the ranks of "labour" to ruin the country and leave it defenceless to the world.'[21] Churchill saw even greater threats than this:

that the strikes were symptomatic of the growth of syndicalism, which would foment social revolution if unchecked. His fears were reinforced by warnings from the mayors of Liverpool and Birkenhead that revolution was imminent, and by the request from the civil authorities of Salford for the despatch of troops.

That workers should be able and willing to challenge the social order was unacceptable to Churchill: 'Militant trade unionism thundered the language of class conflict, forecasting the imminent breakdown of the existing social and economic order. Churchill reacted in kind.'[22] He was not alone in fearing the onset of chaos: the summer's events had 'convinced respectable opinion that the world was about to be turned upside down'.[23] Nevertheless, Churchill's actions still attracted more controversy than those of other ministers, as his responses became increasingly heavy-handed. He continued to use the threat of force against strikers, despatching a cruiser to Liverpool after the death of one man, and stationing 25,000 soldiers just outside London during the dockers' strike. This latter dispute ended peacefully and Churchill wrongly concluded that the presence of troops had persuaded the unions back to the negotiating table – so when an unprecedented national railway strike was threatened he had no hesitation in deploying troops again. This time, however, instead of waiting for requests from the civil authorities, as had happened earlier, Churchill authorised the use of the army himself, thus unilaterally sweeping away the Army Regulation. At the time, the Cabinet had supported his actions, reeling from the ferocity of the strikers' antagonism. But when two strikers were shot and killed at Llanelli by soldiers of the Worcestershire Regiment on 19 August, this decision became instantly controversial. The strike was averted not by Churchill's troops but by Lloyd George's negotiation.

He may have been, as Robbins has claimed, 'not unsympathetic to the aspirations of trade unionists or suffragettes but he would not allow them to dictate the appropriate responses to their grievances'.[24] Or, more clearly, 'he was not prepared to suffer the dictates from below that threatened the social order he held dear'.[25] At heart he was an aristocrat, a privileged member of society. He may have had a genuine desire to improve the conditions of the poor but his progressivism was limited. His innate paternalism was revealed in his reactions to 'the many alarms of a strangely troubled period, in which the rage of the suffragettes coincided with the "great industrial unrest" of 1910–1914'.[26] The coming together of these serious protests would have thrown any Home Secretary into the political limelight, but it seemed to many observers that Churchill enjoyed the confrontations too much. Addison has written of his 'two faces' as Home Secretary: his repressive, paternalistic face that he turned towards the various protestors of the time, and his liberal face. His reputation before becoming Home Secretary had been as a radical reformer and he had entered that office intent on a programme of prison reform. This programme was also not without its controversies.

With his 'strong sense of natural justice, and sympathy for the under-dog'[27] Churchill set about an improvement of conditions for prisoners, reducing sentences to fit the crime committed, reducing the amount of time new prisoners had to spend in solitary confinement, and abolishing the practice of preventive detention, by which re-offenders' sentences could be extended by five to ten years, just to keep them in jail longer. These measures attracted criticism, as did his release of some prisoners simply because he disagreed with the severity of their sentences. Perhaps more controversial still were his ideas on the treatment of the 'feeble-minded'. The idea that such people posed a threat to society's genetic integrity was widespread among some intellectuals of the time, although not among Churchill's Cabinet colleagues. He, however, was enthusiastic about the idea that mentally and physically disabled people could and should be sterilised and segregated, 'so that their curse dies with them'.[28] His attempts to interest his colleagues in possible legislation along these lines failed and although a bill was eventually made law in 1913, this Mental Deficiency Act did not mention sterilisation at all. So even without the strikes and protests that defined Churchill's period at the Home Office, he was willing to propose legislation that aroused controversy with colleagues and the press alike.

This period was a turning point in his career: the point at which his previous social radicalism appeared to fall away, revealing instead an authoritarian figure. Among the working class he lost his reputation as ally to that of enemy, a reputation he was not to begin to shake off until the Second World War. This unmasking coincided with, and may even have contributed to, the loss of support for the Liberal Party among this same group of people, and thus to that party's long decline. The depth of feeling that Churchill's actions aroused was perhaps a matter of positioning – as he was the minister responsible for law and order at a time when it was being subverted by an unusually large number of people – but is more attributable to his enjoyment of controversy. It was noted that he savoured a political fight and was at his most energetic and ebullient when confronted. This was a characteristic that most Liberal ministers did not appreciate, feeling it to be more suited to a barracks than to Whitehall, and this was to have grave consequences for Churchill. From 1910 he had begun to lose friends and political allies, a fact that was to cost him dear during the crisis over Gallipoli in 1915.

Questions

1. In what ways did the Liberal government's attempts to implement social reform cause conflict with the House of Lords?
2. How effective was the partnership of Churchill and Lloyd George in reviving Liberal fortunes in the years 1908–1911?

SOURCES

1. THE SIEGE OF SIDNEY STREET

Source A: Winston Churchill wrote about his role in the Siege of Sidney Street

I thought it my duty to see what was going on myself and my advisers concurred in the propriety of such a step. I must, however, admit that convictions of duty were supported by a strong sense of curiosity which perhaps it would have been well to keep in check ... But the situation almost immediately became embarrassing. Some of the police officers were anxious to storm the building at once with their pistols. Others rightly thought it better to take more time and to avoid the almost certain loss of three or four valuable lives. It was no part of my duty to take personal control or to give executive decisions. From my chair in the Home Office I could have sent any order and it would have been immediately acted on, but it was not for me to interfere with those who were in charge on the spot. Yet, on the other hand, my position of authority, far above them all, attracted inevitably to itself direct responsibility. I saw now that I should have done much better to have remained quietly in my office. On the other hand, it was impossible to get into one's car and drive away while matters stood in such great uncertainty and moreover were extremely interesting ... At about half-past one a wisp of smoke curled out of the shattered upper windows of the besieged house, and in a few minutes it was plainly on fire ... Suddenly, with a stir and a clatter, up came the fire brigade, scattering the crowds ... The inspector of police forbade further progress, and the fire brigade officer declared it his duty to advance. A fire was raging and he was bound to extinguish it. When the police officer pointed out that his men would be shot down, he replied simply that orders were orders ... I now intervened to settle this dispute, at one moment quite heated. I told the fire-brigade officer on my authority as Home Secretary that the house was to be allowed to burn down and that he was to stand by in readiness to prevent the conflagration from spreading.

Source B: from a letter to *The Times*, 6 January 1911

Sir – . . . The fact that two desperate villains 'held up' a whole district of the East-end for many hours on Tuesday last will not easily be forgotten anywhere . . . It is not only a red terror, but a grave peril . . . of bad omen for organized society not only in the East-end, but throughout the Kingdom.

What is essential and what must be at once considered is the necessity of purging the country of this particular type of imported criminal.

Source C: from a letter to *The Times* from 'A MAGISTRATE', 6 January 1911

Are we to gather from the assembling of the King's troops to arrest two desperate ruffians in the East-end of London that the arm of the civil law is so paralysed as to be unable to do what it has done upon many former occasions – viz., arrest without fuss or advertisement . . . ? . . . Sir, I venture to think in former times we managed these things better, and that, if cinematograph pictures of Cabinet ministers are called for by the exigency of modern political life, better opportunities occur than an enterprise which should have been conducted in the sure, swift and successful methods by which our police have in times past vindicated the law.

Source D: from a letter to *The Times* from a member of the National Liberal Club, 10 January 1911

Sir, – it is much regretted that so many of your correspondents are seeking in the deplorable Stepney tragedy an opportunity to attack the Home Secretary. Surely when an affray between the police and criminals has reached such a state as to cause the summoning of soldiers, it is the duty of the Home Secretary, who is responsible to Parliament, to acquaint himself with all the details of the affair . . . Would it have been said that while an unprecedented affray was taking place in the streets of London, while soldiers were firing volleys down a metropolitan thoroughfare, the Home Secretary was lounging in unconcered luxury in Eccleston-Square? Rather than criticize, the public should rejoice in the possession of a Minister whose view of his duty leads him to put up with risk and inconvenience rather than rely for his knowledge of an important occurrence upon the statements of others.

Questions

1.   What does Source A reveal about the influence of Churchill's character on his actions at Sidney Street? (3)
2.   What problems face historians using Source A as evidence of Churchill's role during the siege? (5)

3. Read Sources B and C: using these and your own knowledge, explain why the Siege of Sidney Street raised a number of wider political concerns among the public. (5)
4. Compare Sources C and D: explain how and why they differ in attitude towards Churchill's conduct during the siege. (5)
5. Violet Bonham Carter, a close associate of Churchill's at this time, wrote of the siege that: 'it is one of the most characteristic and revealing episodes of his life'. How completely does this episode reveal the strengths and weaknesses of Churchill as Home Secretary? (12)

Worked Answer

4. Source C is scathing of Churchill's appearance at Sidney Street as being motivated by the desire to appear in 'cinematograph pictures', rather than to bring the siege to a swift conclusion. This source was written by a magistrate, and is, therefore, especially concerned by the apparent inability to bring the siege to a more peaceful, and less public, end. Source D originates from the National Liberal Club and so could be expected to be more sympathetic to Churchill. It takes the view that the siege was an 'unprecedented affray', requiring not just an armed police presence but also the calling in of troops, and that Churchill's presence was evidence of how seriously he took his duties as Home Secretary. Rather than 'lounging in unconcerned luxury' at a London club, he was willing to 'put up with risk and inconvenience' to ensure he was at the scene. For the author of Source D, 'the public should rejoice' that Churchill was the kind of minister to take an active part in attending to such a significant crime.

2. THE TWO FACES OF CHURCHILL AS HOME SECRETARY

Source E: Violet Bonham Carter, writing about Churchill as a Liberal

I could not guess at this time that except for ... these early years in the Liberal Party he would only be really happy and at ease in coalition governments. Though a natural partisan he was never a party politician ... Throughout his life he was never the orthodox mouthpiece of the voice of any ready-made doctrine ... The Tory Party would have seemed to be his natural home. But despite his historic sense of tradition he was untrammelled by convention. Despite his romantic feeling for the aristocracy his broad humanity transcended the boundaries of class. His intensely individual and adventurous mind, for ever on the move, could never be contained by the Conservatives and its questioning, restless brilliance often filled them with an unconcealed disquiet. But though a democrat to the bone, imbued with a deep reverence for Parliament, and a strong sense of human rights, he was never quite a Liberal. He never shared the reluctance which inhibits Liberals from invoking force to solve a problem. And though he revelled in discussion he was by temperament an intellectual aristocrat. He never liked having other people's way. He infinitely preferred his own.

Source F: an historian assesses Churchill's reputation as Home Secretary, in *Churchill: The End of Glory*, published in 1993

Strikes by the Miners' Union over pay and conditions resulted in a shutdown of the pits and, during the picketing which followed, there were confrontations between the police and the miners. The Chief Constable, fearing a breakdown of law and order, asked Whitehall whether troops could be despatched to the coalfields. Churchill saw no need for the employment of the military, a view shared by Haldane [Minister for War]. But it transpired that troops had been sent on the night of the Chief Constable's request by the general officer in command of the southern region. The two Ministers decided to keep the troops back, . . . sending in extra policemen from the Metropolitan force. But the incident provided Churchill with an example of why the Home Office has often been a thankless position to hold. On the one hand, *The Times* criticised him for interfering with the 'arrangements demanded by the Chief Constable' and employing the 'rosewater of conciliation'. On the other side, the episode went down in labour demonology as the occasion upon which Churchill called the troops at Tonypandy.

Source G: an extract from Paul Addison, *Churchill on the Home Front*, on the 'two faces' of Churchill as Home Secretary

Churchill saw himself as a humane and radical statesman, pursuing the course he had marked out at the Board of Trade. 'I am one of those', he said in January 1910, 'who believe that the world is going to get better and better.' Much of his work at the Home Office bore witness to the sincerity of this conviction. His ambitious programme of penal reform, though never completed, marked the pinnacle of his achievement in social policy. But Churchill's great desire to go down in history as a great reforming Home Secretary was overtaken, in the end, by events which turned his political personality around to reveal the other side of paternalism: the maintenance of paternal authority. The Home Secretary was responsible for the preservation of law and order. By chance, Churchill's period at the Home Office coincided with a major outbreak of industrial unrest, accompanied by riots and the risk of violent action between the trade unionists and strike-breaking workers. In the circumstances, any Home Secretary would have taken firm action to quell disorder. Nor was Churchill the melodramatic villain of left-wing tradition, sending in the troops to shoot the strikers. But unlike many politicians, he never shrank from conflict when he believed that an issue had to be resolved.

Source H: *The Times*, 9 November 1910, on Churchill's decision to stop troops before they reached Tonypandy

Yesterday it appears both cavalry and infantry were despatched by train for South Wales, but were stopped at Swindon in consequence of a consultation between the HOME SECRETARY and MR HALDANE. It was thought preferable to send more police instead and to hold back the troops. The HOME SECRETARY took upon himself a grave responsibility in interfering with the arrangements demanded by the CHIEF CONSTABLE ... The renewed rioting late last night seems to have been of a most determined character, and if loss of life occurs, which we fear is more than possible, the responsibility will lie with the HOME SECRETARY. MR CHURCHILL hardly seems to understand that an acute crisis has arisen, which needs decisive handling.

Source I: extract from *The Times'* editorial, 21 November 1910, commenting on the trial of suffragette protestors, following 'Black Friday'

What does the HOME SECRETARY mean? When the first case was called on, MR MUSKETT, who appeared for the prosecution, made the amazing announcement that the HOME SECRETARY had considered the matter, and had come to the conclusion that no public advantage would be gained by continuing the proceedings: ... It is difficult to say what aspect of this incident is the strangest ... It is a novelty, and not one to be welcomed, to intervene in this manner and to stop a prosecution in respect of offences serious and repeated ... Does not this intervention somewhat unsettle ordinary ideas as to punishment?

Questions

1. Read Source E. What light does this author shed on Churchill's character and, therefore, on his likely attitude to problems of law and order? (3)
2. Why, according to the author of Source G, was Churchill's record as Home Secretary bound to be controversial? (5)
3. Compare Sources H and I. How useful are they to a historian assessing Churchill's record as Home Secretary? (5)
4. Read Sources F and H. To what extent do these Sources differ in their interpretation of Churchill's actions at Tonypandy? (5)
5. Using the evidence from all of the Sources, and your own

knowledge, explain the assessment that Churchill 'embodied both the reforming and the conservative potential of the last Liberal Government'. (12)

Worked answer

2. The author of Source G writes that Churchill's tenure as Home Secretary was likely to be controversial for several reasons. First, his years in this office 'coincided with a major outbreak of industrial unrest', resulting in violent clashes between strikers, strike-breakers and the police. Thus Churchill was faced with a succession of crises that, as the minister responsible for law and order, he had to take responsibility for diffusing. However, as Addison points out, Churchill 'never shrank from conflict'. He was convinced of the need to resolve the problems that had led to this unrest by negotiation, but also by force if all else had failed. Addison refers, in this excerpt, to Churchill's 'paternalism' and points out that his willingness to deploy force was simply the flip side of his commitment to reform, both of these impulses inspired by his belief that the people needed to be governed and guided from above for their own good. Churchill also had 'ambitious' plans for penal reform which would probably have courted controversy too, had he had the time to complete them.

2

WARMONGER, 1911–1915

BACKGROUND NARRATIVE

This period was the most tumultuous of Churchill's long and chequered career. It began with his appointment as First Lord of the Admiralty, a post he accepted with alacrity and one he enjoyed thoroughly. The Agadir Crisis of July 1911 opened his eyes to the dangers of the European situation, at which point he dropped all his former objections to higher military spending. Indeed, quarrels with Lloyd George over his increased naval estimates severely strained their political relationship, and was viewed as just one indication of a growing conflict with some Liberal policies. Further evidence of this shift was his attitude to Irish Home Rule, the dominating domestic issue of this time. As Ireland was arming itself for civil war Churchill visited Belfast in 1912, causing a riot in the process, to speak in support of the government's legislation. But his sympathies for the Unionists were always a cause for suspicion among his Liberal colleagues. It was not until his willingness to use force during the Curragh 'mutiny' in 1914 that some of his colleagues were convinced of his support for the settlement. Naturally this episode also aroused memories of his treatment of strikers only the year before, reaffirming his growing reputation as an authoritarian.

However, his more liberal tendency caused him to secure a modest pay rise for ordinary and able seamen (the first since 1857) and to improve conditions below decks. The most significant of his reforms were to create a naval war staff at the Admiralty to parallel that of the War Office and to convert all Royal Navy vessels from coal to oil. This latter decision was taken to secure superiority of speed over the German Navy, but in choosing Anglo-Persian Oil as the supplier, and by buying the majority of its shares, Churchill committed the British government to yet another sphere of influence, in Persia, which would have to be defended. His greatest achievement was that the fleet was ready for war in 1914.

Churchill's fall from power, precipitated by crises over the Gallipoli campaign and the shell shortage, plunged him into despair. His arrogant and ruthless use of his power had won him no friends at the Admiralty or in Parliament. Ostracised, he enlisted, spending six months at the front. He returned in 1916, hoping to return to political life in the Coalition government of his old ally, Lloyd George. But his path was blocked by both Tories and Liberals. Perhaps his partial exoneration with the publication of the Dardanelles Commission Report in March 1917 smoothed his path back into government, although Lloyd George also recognised that an energy as great as Churchill's should be harnessed to, not against, the government. And so Churchill's career was revived with his appointment as Minister of Munitions in July 1917. He attacked the job with characteristic vigour so that after the Coalition's victory in the general election at the end of 1918, he stood poised to take office in Lloyd George's first peacetime administration.

ANALYSIS (1): TO WHAT EXTENT CAN CHURCHILL BE HELD RESPONSIBLE FOR THE FAILURE OF THE DARDANELLES CAMPAIGN?

The failed naval campaign in the Dardanelles and the subsequent futile attempts to take the Gallipoli peninsula in 1915 haunted the rest of Churchill's political life. The entire campaign was judged to be badly planned, poorly coordinated and timidly executed. Churchill was identified as its strongest advocate, so when it failed so dismally, he took the blame. The failure of the first landings at Gallipoli in April 1915 led directly to his ousting from the Admiralty. As the campaign was reduced to stalemate he was forced out of government altogether and resigned his parliamentary seat in November 1915. The issue of Churchill's responsibility for the failure of the campaign has been muddied by the high emotion the campaign itself aroused at the time, by the findings of the Dardanelles Commission, and by Churchill's own explanations of the affair.

The plan to wrest control of the Dardanelles – the narrow channel that links the Black Sea to the Mediterranean – was initially a purely naval one. Using old battleships, the Dardanelles would be 'forced' by a slow, methodical bombardment of its defensive forts on land. It was assumed that the forts were so old they would crumble easily, and that once under attack the Ottoman Empire would capitulate. It was only as the bombardment began that Kitchener offered troops. Therefore, it was only a naval campaign, not a joint campaign with the War Office, which Churchill had planned and presented to colleagues for approval. His enthusiasm for it stemmed from several important considerations and assumptions, which he believed outweighed the risks that were involved.

His major concern was one he shared with a number of his Cabinet colleagues and which posed a threat to their unity. By the end of 1914 the Western Front had reached stalemate. To some ministers the front's insatiable need for men and ammunition seemed an extraordinary waste, given that no progress was being made. The idea that the war would be won only by killing more German soldiers than they killed British and French (a war of attrition) was repugnant to many politicians. Thus one group of ministers, Lloyd George and Churchill included, had begun to search for alternatives. So while the 'westerners' continued to clamour for more supplies for France, the 'easterners' looked to other regions of Europe from which to launch another attack on Germany and her Allies. On the outbreak of war, Churchill was quickly convinced that the Ottomans would soon drop their neutrality in favour of Germany, an opinion strengthened when they closed the Dardanelles to all shipping in September 1914. He advocated a pre-emptive attack and put his thoughts to Prime Minister Asquith in December 1914: 'Are there not other alternatives than sending our armies to chew barbed wire in Flanders? Further, cannot the power of the Navy be brought more directly to bear upon the enemy?'[1]

Clearly Churchill's motivation for supporting an alternative theatre of war can be ascribed to his frustration with the lack of progress on the Western Front, but many also suspected him of wanting to spearhead a large naval campaign for his own ambitions. Nevertheless, his plan for a naval assault on the Dardanelles was accepted in principle, and was unopposed by the War Council on 13 January 1915. The War Council had been set up to deal with the issues arising from being at war and consisted of a mixture of Cabinet ministers, senior military advisers from the War Office and Admiralty, and Arthur Balfour, leader of the opposition. Although it met less often than the Cabinet, it was responsible for taking all decisions on the conduct of the war. Churchill's plan was a very brief proposal, written at his request by the admiral stationed in the Mediterranean, and was not detailed. Yet it was approved by the War Council as viable, without reference to either maps or military intelligence of the area to be attacked. It has been argued that Churchill practically bullied the War Council into accepting the plan and that 'there can be little doubt but for his unrelenting pressure, it would never have been undertaken'.[2]

However, 'Churchill was not alone in believing that the Dardanelles were a short cut to victory',[3] and the rewards for a successful campaign were rich and tempting. In knocking the Ottomans out of the war and seizing control of the Dardanelles (the rapid defeat of 'the sick man of Europe' was taken for granted at this stage), Britain would have been able to send vital supplies to Russia all year round via the warm-water ports of the Black Sea, and thus help to sustain her faltering war effort on the Eastern Front. In addition it was assumed that in taking the offensive in the Balkans, its neutral states, such as Greece, Bulgaria and Romania, would have been persuaded to join the Entente. These political possibilities outweighed the military considerations so that the plan was unanimously approved.

Churchill later claimed that 'the genesis of this plan and its elaboration were purely naval and professional in their character'.[4] This stretches the truth somewhat. By the time that the War Council had authorised the campaign to go ahead, he had discussed it with only a select few. The Admiralty Board, Sea Lords who should have acted as expert advisers, had not been consulted. Only Fisher, the First Sea Lord, had talked it over with Churchill in any detail, although Fisher's lack of honesty in these discussions caused Churchill much trouble later. In presenting the plan to the War Council as one that the whole Admiralty had agreed, Churchill himself was less than honest, and inadvertently sowed the seeds of his own downfall. The Dardanelles Commission (established to investigate the reasons for the campaign's failure) reported that: 'It is clear that Mr Asquith was ill-informed as regards the methods under which Admiralty business was conducted'.[5] Churchill's lack of candour had grave consequences, for it contributed to the ease with which a flawed plan was implemented, at the cost, eventually, of many lives.

In fact, the naval bombardment came tantalisingly close to success on 18 March 1915; so much so that offers of troops for the campaign were made by France and Greece, and in the USA grain prices fell dramatically in the expectation that soon the Dardanelles would be open to shipping and Russian grain would flood the market. That the advantages gained on 18 March were not pursued to victory was not Churchill's doing. It was at this point that he lost all direct control over the campaign. The commanding officer on the spot, De Roebuck, had been shaken by the loss on that day of three battleships to mines. He decided to postpone further bombardment until the channel could be swept. This postponement was then extended to await the arrival of the troops, lately promised by Kitchener, to the region, so as to coordinate a landed assault with further shelling of the forts. The decision meant a delay of at least three weeks, but there were further problems and the landed assault did not take place until 25 April. None of these decisions can be attributed to Churchill since they were taken with little reference to his wishes, but with much to those of Kitchener.

Having first denied that any troops could be sent to support the naval attack, he had agreed that the 29th Division could be despatched to the Aegean at a War Council meeting of 9 February. But on the 19th Kitchener again changed his mind and retracted this commitment, only to announce on 10 March that the 29th Division would go after all. Of this Churchill later wrote, 'The workings of Lord Kitchener's mind constituted at this period a feature almost as puzzling as the great war problem itself . . . The repeated changes of plan were baffling in the last degree.'[6] Kitchener's domination of the War Council explains the fact that it accepted, without question, his unilateral decision to convert what had been a purely naval assault to a combined one, and allowed the campaign orders for the landings to be given out without having seen or discussed them first. He had dominated the War Council since its establishment in 1914 when he had been appointed Secretary of State for War. His public reputation was immense, having been Commander-in-Chief during the Boer War and served in both India and Egypt – cornerstones of the British Empire. His apparent imperturbability together with the flash of inspiration that led him to declare the war would be long, not over by Christmas, and to recruit the largest army yet raised in Britain, added to his reputation of infallibility. In appointing him, Asquith had hoped to instil confidence in the leadership of the war. But Kitchener has been described as 'Autocratic in manner and disdainful of politicians',[7] qualities which did not bode well for the smooth running of an experimental government in which military and civilian leaders would work in tandem.

His influence was made all the greater by the fact that the War Council itself was flawed in its operation. Its procedures were ill defined, minutes of meetings were kept but not circulated or agreed by the participants, and the military members believed that their role was to speak only when spoken to. This meant that members could leave a meeting without any clear idea of whether a decision had been reached, or whether everyone supported it. That its members were to be collectively responsible for its decisions is a mockery in the light of these serious flaws. The Dardanelles Commission reported that 'the atmosphere of vagueness and want of precision which seems to have characterised the proceedings of the War Council'[8] contributed to the difficulties of the Dardanelles campaign, in its inception, refinement and prosecution. The Commission did not feel it appropriate to comment on Kitchener's role in the campaign as he was the only one of the main protagonists who was no longer alive to put his case, and his reputation among the public was still high. But A. J. P. Taylor has argued that his lack of strategic skill meant that 'civilian ministers were provoked into devising strategy themselves – some of them not at all reluctantly'.[9]

Churchill indeed showed no reluctance when plunging into the planning of a number of military campaigns, of which the Dardanelles had been just one. His ability to become utterly immersed in one issue meant he could always be accused of becoming obsessed to the point of blindness, as he was over the Dardanelles. Working within the flawed system by which strategy was devised and agreed, Churchill's persistence won. Thus in public and political arenas, he was identified as the main protagonist for the campaign; so when it failed he was obviously to blame. Yet it was the land campaign, for which Churchill could take less responsibility than Kitchener, which failed at such high cost. Churchill's naval campaign had resulted in the loss of a handful of battleships, not in thousands of lives. But by May 1915 his fall from power was inevitable. His responsibility for the failure of the Dardanelles campaign mattered less than the way in which he had gone about securing its approval. Both his Liberal colleagues and Conservatives had grown to distrust his motivation and methods, so that when his First Sea Lord, Fisher, resigned on the same day that news broke of the shell supply crisis to the Western Front, his position was very vulnerable. While Kitchener's reputation remained intact (in public, at least) his position in the government remained unassailable. But some dramatic change of personnel was necessary if Asquith was to keep his administration in power and maintain the political truce with the opposition. Neville has commented that 'the total failure of Gallipoli allowed the Tories to demand the head of the most hated member of the Liberal Party'.[10] And that head was Churchill's. Here, after a meteoric, unconventional and controversial rise to power, was Churchill's come-uppance. He had to pay the price not so much for a weakly planned and executed military campaign but for his willingness to manipulate facts to build his case and his failure to build any support for his case among his military or civilian colleagues.

Questions

1. Should Churchill have been forced from office following the failure of the Dardanelles campaign?
2. What weaknesses in the system of wartime government did the Dardanelles campaign reveal?

ANALYSIS (2): WHAT CAN A COMPARISON OF LLOYD GEORGE AND CHURCHILL REVEAL ABOUT THEIR POLITICAL CAREERS?

'He grappled with the giant events and strove to compel them, undismayed by mistakes and their consequences. Tradition and convention troubled him little.'[11] Churchill wrote this about Lloyd George's leadership during the First World War, but it could have been equally applied to Churchill's. The careers of these two men intertwined for the best part of half a century, sometimes in harmony and sometimes not, so it is fascinating and illuminating to compare the careers of these two giants of early twentieth-century British politics. Apparently unlikely allies, they consistently defied convention throughout their careers, resisting the mould of party politics to suit their own convictions, and redefining the role of the office of Prime Minister.

The most obvious comparison is of their leadership during the two world wars: Lloyd George's during the first and Churchill's in the second. Both men were made Prime Minister not by election but in response to crises of confidence in the government of the time, and both were leaders of coalitions. By this stage in their careers neither man commanded the loyalty of any single political party. Neither could be counted a party politician, being attracted instead to the idea of coalition or of a centre party, even in peacetime. Churchill had attempted to form a centre party as early in his career as 1903, and had supported enthusiastically Lloyd George's suggestion of a coalition in 1910. 'Traditional party loyalties were not sacred to either man, particularly where issues of high national policy, as interpreted by them, were concerned . . . These two great mavericks of modern British politics were both to find final and lasting greatness in coalitions of sorts.'[12] Thus their subsequent positions as leaders of coalitions come as no surprise, since they enabled these two mavericks to work outside the limits of party political programmes.

The similarities run deeper still. As Prime Minister, Lloyd George had to solve the problems of organising a war effort for the first 'total war' in Europe. His success in galvanising and reorganising government departments, and in recruiting entrepreneurs and businessmen to reform certain areas of production, won him the epithet 'the man who won the war'. Churchill wrote of Lloyd George that he 'drove the engine of the State forward at increasing speed'.[13] To create the new ministries necessary for the prosecution of the war – National Service, Labour, Food, Pensions and Shipping, to name but a few – meant breaking with traditional Liberal policies once and for all. The issue of conscription was the most controversial, but the general extension of the state's powers into areas of economic, industrial and employment policy was a difficult necessity for some traditional Liberals to accept. Breaking tradition was something that both Lloyd George and Churchill were unafraid to do. Once Prime Minister, Churchill reaped the rewards of Lloyd George's inventiveness, as the government was able to put itself on a war footing much more quickly, by building on the experience of the First World War. Both men galvanised a civil service notoriously slow to change, and stories of previously staid civil servants seen running along the corridors of Whitehall are common to both Lloyd George's and Churchill's leaderships. That Churchill had admired the qualities of Lloyd George's leadership is obvious from the following comment: 'Every day for him was filled with the hope and the impulse of a fresh beginning . . . This inexhaustible mental agility, guided by the main purpose of Victory, was a rare advantage.'[14] Once again this could equally have been written of Churchill in 1940–1945.

More particularly, Lloyd George's relationship with the military proved of great significance for Churchill's leadership during the Second World War. The conflict between the 'Frocks and Brasshats' of the first war dominated its course. Asquith had tried to solve the puzzle of ensuring that military strategy was both professionally devised by the army and subject to scrutiny by democratic bodies such as the Cabinet by appointing Field Marshal Kitchener as Secretary of State for War in 1914. This only added to the difficulties, and the experiment was brought to an end by Kitchener's sudden death at sea in June 1916. Lloyd George made a number of attempts to establish greater control over the military after the failure of Haig's summer offensive in 1917. First, he intentionally starved the front of troops as a way to limit Haig's plans. Second, he established a body, the Supreme War Council, to supersede him in November 1917, at which the British, French and Italian prime ministers would meet to coordinate strategy themselves. Finally, he agreed to the appointment in April 1918 of the French Marshal Foch as Supreme

Commander of the allied armies on the Western Front, to whom Haig was subordinated. Lloyd George's own lack of military knowledge had handicapped his ability to govern the military aspects of the war satisfactorily.

Churchill understood this well, and was much better qualified in military matters. Thus, upon becoming Prime Minister in May 1940, he also appointed himself Minister of Defence. He did not define the powers of this new office, but it meant that he could do two things that Lloyd George had not been able to do: assume direct and daily contact, control and authority over the military, and exclude the civilian service ministers from the War Cabinet. These two measures had the effect of streamlining the process of leading the war effort. Churchill chaired the meetings of the military Chiefs of Staff himself, and it was there that strategy was discussed and formed. The War Cabinet, following Lloyd George's model, included ministers who had no departmental responsibilities and so devoted their whole attention to policies and decisions at the highest level of the war effort. This structure concentrated a great deal of power in Churchill's hands – more power than any British Prime Minister has had before or since. As a man who had great confidence in his military expertise, Churchill was able to challenge and formulate strategy, a fact that had its own problems, but which gave him greater control and direction than Lloyd George had achieved.

He recognised, as did Lloyd George, that war called for extraordinary measures, writing in 1923, 'In war everything is different. There is no place for compromise in war . . . Clear leadership, violent action, rigid decisions one way or the other, form the only path not only of victory, but of safety and even of mercy.'[15] When transferred to peacetime politics, this approach did not always produce such positive results as it did during wartime. Churchill was often accused of being interfering, auto-cratic and arrogant, and of trying to accrue too much power – qualities that were unwelcome during peacetime, but beneficial in wartime. Similarly, Lloyd George's 'presidential' style of leadership was well suited to leading the war effort, but was quickly resented once the war was over. Their reforming zeal was influential during their first collaboration in the pre-war Liberal government. As the 'heavenly twins' of New Liberalism, their vigorous pursuit of social reform revived the party for a time, but eventually proved too divisive. The People's Budget of 1909, conceived by Lloyd George and supported by Churchill as a way to finance social reform by taxing the rich, led to the constitutional crisis of 1910. However, as Chancellor of the Exchequer and President of the Board of Trade, Lloyd George and Churchill were 'allies in laying the foundations of what came later to be known as the welfare state'.[16]

Between them they created a system of pensions and health care for workers in certain trades, despite initial opposition from all quarters.

Their energy and ingenuity were astonishing. This, coupled with their ability to pick and choose policies whether they were part of party doctrine or not, and their imagination and intellect, meant that they were a formidable pair. They did not always work in tandem, notably falling out over naval estimates when Churchill was at the Admiralty and Lloyd George was at the Treasury, for example, yet they shaped every office they held. As Chancellors, both men displayed not only their oratorical skills when livening up the budget day speech, but their ability to think creatively. While Lloyd George financed both increased naval expenditure and new state pension schemes in his famous budget of 1909, Churchill foresaw the revenue potential of placing a tax on petrol sales in his 1928 budget, using the income to part-finance a reorganisation of local government. In 1928 Neville Chamberlain wrote of Churchill, 'He seeks instinctively for the large and preferably novel idea such as is capable of representation by the broadest brush.'[17] This ability to think in the broadest terms meant that they were both radicals seeking fundamental, not piecemeal, change.

The emphasis on social policy and reform was to remain with Lloyd George as a constant aim. His rewriting of the Liberal Party's political programme in the 1920s demonstrates his continued agitation for improved standards of living, housing and employment for the working classes; the titles of the so-called 'coloured books' reveal the importance of these concerns to him – *The Land and the Nation* of 1925 and *We Can Conquer Unemployment* of 1929, for example. For Churchill, the same cannot quite be said. His early career as a Liberal minister was the only period in which social policy was his main focus. However, the influence of his mentor appeared to follow him even after he had rejoined the Conservatives. Some concern for certain social policies was evident during his time as Chancellor of the Exchequer. Of his 1925 budget Jenkins writes, 'He was determined to present the budget . . . as a "condition of the people" enterprise, well in the tradition of his pre-1914 partnership with Lloyd George.'[18] During the Second World War, however, he devolved practically all questions of social policy to Sir John Anderson's committee and referred to him as his domestic Prime Minister. At the end of the war, 'Churchill plainly failed to appreciate the importance attached by the electorate to such issues as housing and employment policy'[19] and lost the general election of July 1945.

However, Lloyd George's success in retaining office after the First World War was tarnished by the failure to deliver his promise to build a 'country fit for heroes to live in'. Perhaps even this had an effect on

Churchill, for although he did not learn this lesson – that domestic policies would take precedence over international affairs during peacetime – the electorate did. They 'remembered how they had been cheated, or supposed that they had been cheated, after the general election of 1918. Lloyd George brought ruin to Churchill from the grave' in the similar circumstances of 1945.[20]

Perhaps because of this wisdom on the part of the people, Churchill's reputation did not suffer the degradation of Lloyd George's. While the former was held in such high esteem that he was given a state funeral upon his death in 1965 (something usually reserved for members of the royal family), Lloyd George was not. He did not hold office after 1922, although Churchill apparently offered him a position in 1940, and, despite his efforts to revive the fortunes of the Liberal Party, has more often been blamed for dividing it than reforming it. The two men differed above all in 'that Winston knew when he was being unscrupulous, whereas Lloyd George did not.'[21] Both men may have been extremely difficult to work with, temperamental and demanding, but where Churchill was transparent, Lloyd George was devious, and where Churchill could inspire trust, Lloyd George did not.

Questions

1. Why were both Winston Churchill and Lloyd George less successful as peacetime than as wartime Prime Ministers?
2. Why has Churchill's reputation remained high when Lloyd George's has not?

SOURCES

1. THE DARDANELLES CAMPAIGN

Source A: an extract from the First Report of the Dardanelles Commission, published in 1917

There can be no doubt that at the two meetings on January 28th, Mr Churchill strongly advocated the adoption of the Dardanelles enterprise ... We think that, considering what Mr Churchill knew of the opinions entertained by Lord Fisher and Sir Arthur Wilson [Admiral of the Fleet], and considering also the fact that the other experts at the Admiralty who had been consulted, although they assented to an attack on the outer forts of the Dardanelles ..., had not done so with any great cordiality or enthusiasm, he ought, instead of urging Lord Fisher, as he seems to have done at the private meeting after luncheon on January 28th, to give a silent, but manifestly very reluctant, assent to the undertaking, not merely to have invited Lord Fisher and Sir Arthur Wilson to express their views freely to the [War] Council, but further to have insisted on their doing so, in order that the Ministerial members might be placed in full possession of all the arguments for and against the enterprise. We have not the least doubt that, in speaking at the Council, Mr Churchill thought that he was correctly representing the collective views of the Admiralty experts. But, without in any way wishing to impugn his good faith, it seems clear that he was carried away by his sanguine temperament and his firm belief in the success of the undertaking which he advocated. Although none of his expert advisers absolutely expressed dissent, all the evidence laid before us leads us to the conclusion that Mr Churchill had obtained their support to a less extent than he himself imagined.

Source B: Churchill wrote the following about the episode in *The World Crisis*, published in 1923

Upon me more than any other person the responsibility for the Dardanelles and all that it involved has been cast. Upon me fell almost exclusively the fierce war-time censures of Press and Public. Upon me alone among the high authorities concerned was the penalty inflicted – not of loss of office, for that is a petty thing – but of interruption and deprivation of control while the fate of the enterprise was still in suspense . . . as will be seen, I accept the fullest responsibility for all that I did and had the power to do.

Source C: Churchill writing about Lord Fisher's withdrawal of support for the Dardanelles plan, in *The World Crisis*

I am in no way concealing the great and continuous pressure which I put upon the old Admiral. This pressure was reinforced by Lord Kitchener's personal influence, by the collective opinion of the War Council, and by the authoritative decision of the Prime Minister . . . Was it wrong to put this pressure upon the First Sea Lord? I cannot think so. War is a business of terrible pressures, and persons who take part in it must fail if they are not strong enough to withstand them. As a mere politician and civilian, I would never have agreed to the Dardanelles project if I had not believed in it . . . Had I been in Lord Fisher's position and held his views, I would have refused point blank . . . First Sea Lords have to stand up to facts and take their decisions resolutely.

Source D: extract from 'The Gallipoli Memorial Lecture', given by Robert O'Neill, 1990

By early November 1914 it was clear that the traditional Cabinet system was in difficulty in conducting a major war. Churchill's order to bombard the Turkish forts at the entrance to the Dardanelles was given without Cabinet discussion, yet it was a major act of policy which carried consequences rightly called ... 'far-reaching and unfortunate' ... The key decisions regarding the escalation of the attack to the level of a major amphibious operation were taken piecemeal by three men, Churchill, Kitchener and Asquith, who failed properly to examine the real difficulty of what they were attempting and the implications of meeting stout resistance ... Churchill was culpable in several ways. He played a dominant role in a slipshod decision-making process. He manipulated the words of his subordinates such as the unfortunate Admiral Carden in order to get his way with Asquith and Kitchener. He bulldozed everyone from the Prime Minister through to Carden and de Roebuck to ensure his wishes were translated into action. Yet he did the nation and the Empire a service in hatching a brilliant alternative strategy. Abortive though the Dardanelles offensive proved, it was none the less the right sort of alternative to look for. The ultimate cause of the tragedy that we commemorate tonight was the lack of tough-minded, confident, well-informed people at Cabinet level who would criticise Churchill's ideas as he formed them. For want of critics one of Britain's best strategic minds led the Empire to disaster.

Source E: one of the historians of the Gallipoli campaign, Robert Rhodes James, assesses Churchill's responsibility for its failure

Its 'genesis' lay entirely with Churchill. His eyes had been on the Dardanelles from the moment that Turkish intervention on the German side appeared probable; he had been the first to call for professional views on the military problems involved in an attack on the Gallipoli Peninsula; he had been the first to urge such an operation ... While it is reasonable for Churchill's admirers to applaud his strategic genius, it is hardly reasonable for them, almost in the same breath, to cast the burden of failure upon his advisers. This does not excuse Fisher and his colleagues for their responsibility ... But the impelling force was Churchill's; the initiative was solely his; and the responsibility for what ensued must be principally his.

Questions

1. Read Source A. What is the main criticism in this Source of Churchill's conduct in pressing the War Council to adopt the Dardanelles plan? (3)
2. How useful are Sources B and C to a historian assessing Churchill's role in the decision to implement the Dardanelles plan? (5)
3. To what extent do Sources D and E disagree in their interpretation of Churchill's responsibility for the decision to attack the Dardanelles? (5)

4. Using Source C and your own knowledge, explain the significance of Churchill's reference to himself as a 'mere politician and civilian'. (5)
5. 'There can be little doubt that but for his unrelenting pressure, it would never have been undertaken.' Using the evidence of all the Sources, and your own knowledge, to what extent do you agree with this statement? (12)

Worked answer

4. Churchill's use of these words is significant. This Source is an extract from his book *The World Crisis*, which was published in 1923, and in which Churchill was able to 'put his case' in the debate over responsibility for the Dardanelles campaign. Churchill argued that although he accepted full responsibility for the decisions that he took, there were others, particularly the military advisers, who should also have taken some responsibility. He refers to both Kitchener and Fisher in this Source, pointing out that they too had participated in the decisions that led to the Dardanelles campaign. He also argues that had he been a military expert, as these two were, and had he disagreed with the plan, as Fisher did, he would have spoken out against it. Churchill was angered by Fisher's late rejection of the plan and the latter's claims that he had never supported it in the first place. He also believed that it had made his political survival impossible. In making such a pointed reference to his being a 'mere politician and civilian' he was confirming his view that he had not been well served by his military advisers, whose role was to provide the military expertise a 'mere politician and civilian' needed in order to take the decision to pursue a campaign or not. And he was making it clear that the blame for the campaign should be shared, not shouldered by him alone.

2. CHURCHILL AND LLOYD GEORGE

Source F: an extract from John Charmley's biography, *Churchill: The End of Glory*, published in 1993

The Gladstonian tradition had no remedies for the problems of unemployment, low wages and poverty – which was where the 'new' Liberalism came into its own. With Lloyd George as Chancellor and Churchill at the Board of Trade, Asquith had equipped himself with two Ministers whose eclecticism would avoid the perils of a doctrinaire approach, but who would, by their energy, infuse life into a government which seemed to be running out of steam. The 'heavenly twins' (as the two men came to be known) became a conduit through which the ideas of people like the Webbs were channelled into public life.

Source G: Violet Bonham Carter, Asquith's daughter, in an extract from her book *Winston Churchill as I Knew Him*, published in 1965

Lloyd George was a virtuoso in all the arts of political manipulation and I think his lack of scruple must at times have startled Winston, although he was too dazzled to be shocked. There is no doubt that he was influenced by it. Lloyd George was his senior by eleven years and he saw him as a political 'man of the world' who knew what was done and not done. One difference was that Winston knew when he was being unscrupulous, whereas Lloyd George did not. Winston, on the rare occasions when he attempted to deceive, was so transparent a deceiver that his ultimate sincerity was beyond doubt, whereas Lloyd George's sincerity was often questioned by those who were not under his spell . . . I began to notice a new political inflection in his attitudes and even in his words. I remember saying to him one day, 'You've been talking to Lloyd George.' 'And why shouldn't I?' he replied defensively. 'Of course there's no reason why you shouldn't – but he's "come off" on you. You are talking like him instead of like yourself.' He rebutted this accusation by saying that they saw eye to eye on every subject so of course they spoke alike. He added fervently that Lloyd George was a man of genius, the greatest political genius he had ever met.

Source H: Norman Rose assesses Lloyd George and Churchill's relationship in 1917

It was not until July 1917 that Lloyd George felt sufficiently secure to bring back Churchill as Minister of Munitions, the job he had sought a year earlier. Even so, Tory ministers vehemently opposed his inclusion in the government; Lloyd George did not allow this criticism to sway his judgement. Not that he was unaware of Churchill's shortcomings . . . But Lloyd George was also deeply conscious of the damage a Churchill hungry for office might provoke in opposition. His own position was by no means secure. The Lloyd George–Churchill partnership was renewed, coloured by its customary mixture of mutual admiration and mistrust.

Source I: the historian Lukacs writing about Churchill's invitation to Lloyd George in 1940 to join the War Cabinet

On the twenty-eighth of May Churchill wrote to Lloyd George, inviting him into the Cabinet. Why did he do this? After all, it was Lloyd George who, after having met Hitler in September 1936 pronounced him as 'the greatest living German'. In October 1939 Lloyd George said openly in Parliament that Hitler's peace offers must be taken seriously . . . On the sixth of June he returned to his idea of inviting Lloyd George into the Cabinet. Churchill had already gone to Chamberlain, asking him to put personal feelings aside and agree to the inclusion of Lloyd George for the sake of national unity. If Lloyd George had remained 'an outcast', he would become a 'focus for regathering discontents' with the war. What is significant in this matter is . . . Churchill's purpose to be able to count upon Lloyd George in the event of a great national crisis. He knew that Lloyd George was a potential spokesman for a compromise peace with Hitler.

Source J: a biographer of Lloyd George compares him with Churchill

But whereas Lloyd George's reflective and imaginative powers were nearly always directly related to immediate practical tasks, Churchill's mind had a brooding . . . quality which enabled him on occasion to anticipate the future with uncanny accuracy – as in his famous prediction that 'the wars of the peoples' would be 'more terrible than those of kings' – but could also lead him into error and folly. If his judgements were sometimes more far-sighted than Lloyd George's, Lloyd George's were often more sensible and realistic. Another difference was that, while both men were equally self-centred in their fundamental approach to life, Lloyd George was less self-regarding . . . Both were brilliant talkers, but Lloyd George, unlike Churchill, was also an excellent listener. Lloyd George revelled in the free trade of conversation and discussion, whereas Churchill was addicted to monologue . . . As a speaker, too, he was more effective than Churchill on public platforms and in Parliament: his voice was more musical and his style . . . appeared more spontaneous. Yet he never mastered the medium of broadcasting, and it was chiefly in that medium that Churchill, during the Second World War, was able to make speeches which had a more profound effect than any others delivered in this century.

Questions

1. Explain the term ' "new" Liberalism' in Source F. (3)
2. What light does Source G shed on the early relationship between Lloyd George and Churchill? (5)
3. Compare Sources G and J. Which of these is the more useful Source for a historian making a comparison of Churchill and Lloyd George? (5)
4. Read Sources H and I. Why, according to these Sources, was it important that neither Lloyd George nor Churchill be excluded from government during periods of national emergency? (5)
5. To what extent do these Sources support the judgement that

'Lloyd George came to be more than a political associate and mentor to Churchill; he became, as well, . . . a surrogate father.' (12)

Worked answer

4. Source H focuses on Lloyd George's decision to take Churchill back into government in 1917 following his downfall after Gallipoli. The Source argues that he did so because 'he was deeply conscious of the damage a Churchill hungry for office might provoke in opposition'. Source I focuses on Churchill's decision to ask Lloyd George to join his War Cabinet in 1940, stimulated by his understanding that 'if Lloyd George had remained "an outcast", he would become "a focus for regathering discontents" with the war.' Both men, then, had a reputation for being important enough that they could not be excluded from power at times of national emergency. Source H points out that Lloyd George's position as the leader of a national coalition 'was by no means secure', whereas Source I reveals the extent to which Churchill was worried about 'national unity', as leader of a national coalition that had also come into existence in response to external threats. Both men demonstrated throughout their careers how disruptive they could be in opposition, and these Sources reveal how well they knew that about each other.

3

CHANCELLOR, 1924–1929

BACKGROUND NARRATIVE

The 'khaki' election of December 1918 returned Lloyd George's coalition to power. Churchill was appointed Secretary of State for War and Air. His first task was to demobilise the largest army in British history, which he did by scrapping existing and unpopular plans, replacing them with a fairer scheme that successfully diffused tensions. It was his suggestion that led to the adoption of the 'Ten Year Rule', in 1919, that military spending be based on an assumption that British forces would not go to war within the next ten years. It was this same rule that led to military spending cuts, which he was to argue against in the 1930s. He presided over the creation of the Royal Air Force as a separate force, convinced as he was that air power was going to change the nature of warfare in the future.

More controversially, Churchill vigorously campaigned for greater allied intervention in the Russian Civil War. He was appalled at the nature of the Bolshevik regime, instinctively disliking its ideology and use of terror. His criticisms were vehement and, some felt, alarmist. His ambitions for further intervention were thwarted by a Britain exhausted by the Great War and facing war in Ireland. Initially, Churchill supported Lloyd George's punitive policies in Ireland, but by 1920 was participating in the negotiations to bring about a settlement. During his tenure as Secretary of State for the Colonies, he successfully steered the controversial legislation for the establishment of the Irish Free State through Parliament, and managed to settle disputed borders in the Middle East.

By 1922 Lloyd George's position as Prime Minister was increasingly challenged by critics of the Irish settlement, and by the threat of war during the 'Chanak Crisis' in August. The Conservatives voted to withdraw from the coalition at a meeting at the Carlton Club in October, forcing the Prime Minister to call an election. The coalition government fell from power and Churchill lost his seat. He didn't enter Parliament again until 1924. Instead he spent his time travelling and painting, lecturing and writing. Politically his drift to the right, noticeable since just before the Great War, continued. The adoption of protectionist policies by the Conservatives in the 1923 general election delayed Churchill's return to them, as he considered himself a free trader. But that election result was decisive for his future: the Conservatives lost and subsequently abandoned protectionism, while the Liberals chose to support the formation of the first Labour government.

Churchill naturally deplored this decision for allowing the 'menace of socialism' to take power. By early 1924 he had negotiated a return to the Conservatives as a 'Constitutionalist'. MacDonald's Labour government did not live long. The general election in October 1924 was dominated by the scandal of the 'Zinoviev letter', which created a hysterical backlash that Churchill was happy to exploit. The Conservatives were returned to government and Churchill to Parliament.

ANALYSIS (1): HOW SUCCESSFUL WAS CHURCHILL AS CHANCELLOR OF THE EXCHEQUER, 1924–1929?

Baldwin's appointment of Churchill as his Chancellor caught everyone, even Churchill, by surprise. In comparison with most of his new Cabinet colleagues he had the most political experience behind him. Yet he was not an economist. This, and the fact that he had been out of political favour since 1922, meant he was more willing than usual to follow orthodox policies. Churchill was anxious to prove to his readopted party that he was politically sound and deserving of their trust.

His first budget confirmed the return to the Gold Standard, valuing the pound at its pre-war rate of £1 to $4.86. At the time, 'the overwhelming consensus of financial opinion was in favour of the return to gold, at pre-war parity'.[1] But this same policy 'is commonly regarded as the greatest mistake of that main Baldwin government, and the responsibility for it came firmly to rest upon Churchill'.[2]

In accepting the arguments in favour of returning to the Gold Standard – and Churchill undertook a thorough investigation into the matter before committing himself – he followed financial orthodoxy and the political consensus of the time. Previous governments had been committed to the principle of returning to the Gold Standard. One of the few exceptions to this consensus was the young economist J. M. Keynes. His pamphlet, 'The Economic Consequences of Mr Churchill', stated that the pound had been overvalued by 10 per cent, and warned this would lead to British exports becoming too expensive. The consequential fall in exports would cause industry to reduce wages and employment in the effort to remain profitable. Keynes was one of only a few dissenters. It wasn't until later, when the expected benefits of returning to the Gold Standard had failed to materialise, that these criticisms were acknowledged as having any basis. Instead of stimulating Britain's stagnant economy, the overvalued pound led to a fall in exports. Jobs were cut and wages forced down as industries struggled to survive, leading to the unrest and strikes that characterised the early years of the Baldwin government.

Churchill took the blame for his fateful decision. He later claimed it had been 'the biggest blunder in his life',[3] but it seems unlikely that he could have done any differently. Most of Britain's main trading partners had returned, or were about to return, their currencies to the Gold Standard. In his final debate with pro- and anti-Gold Standard advisers, conducted over dinner, he came to understand that while the economic consequences of a return were unpredictable, it was politically expected that the country return to the pre-war 'normality' of convertibility with gold. Later economic historians have calculated that had Churchill valued the pound at 10 per cent less than its pre-war value, unemployment could have fallen by as much as 727,000. This failure to reduce unemployment blighted Baldwin's administration, costing it the election of 1929. More immediately it resulted in a dramatic rise in industrial conflict, ruining any chance of good relations with the trade unions.

In particular, the coal industry, in crisis since the end of the war, was devastated by the high exchange rate. Unable to export its coal, the industry threatened wage cuts. The government subsidised the mines while a Royal Commission attempted to find a solution, but in the end was reluctant to intervene in this privately owned industry. Both miners and owners then proved too stubborn to negotiate a settlement themselves. A lockout ensued, other unions came out in support, and Britain's first

General Strike had begun. Churchill had a hand in trying to end the miners' crisis, coming closer than Baldwin to succeeding. His inclination was to be much more conciliatory towards the miners than were his colleagues, believing that 'the country was suffering debilitating economic bleeding and that it was the duty of the government to staunch the flow at the earliest possible moment'.[4] The enormous cost of this, and of the General Strike, was the dominant influence on Churchill's budgets of 1926 and 1927. It was only through some creative thinking and ingenious juggling that he was able to make his budgets appear to balance.

He did this by emptying the Road Fund over two years, ignoring the fact that this money had been set aside for spending on roads. He raised more money to cover the deficits of these two years by introducing a betting tax, increasing taxes on luxury goods, and speeding up the payment dates for brewery taxes. He also insisted on swingeing cuts in naval and army spending, making him very unpopular with some of his Cabinet colleagues. Excepting the immediate post-war years of 1918–1920, Churchill ran the largest budgetary deficit of the inter-war period, at nearly £37 million in the years 1926 and 1927. Yet he also contrived a small decrease in the national debt and in income tax.

More important, though, was the fact that Churchill did not challenge financial orthodoxy. Despite being desperate to find ways to inject life into the economy, he did not intend to run a deficit to adopt a loan-financed programme of public works. Such Keynesian economics were not to be accepted and adopted as national policy until the Second World War. Churchill did come up with a kind of solution: his de-rating scheme announced in his budget of 1928 was intended to stimulate the economy by freeing industry and agriculture from having to pay rates (a tax) to their local authority – the theory being that it would release more money into the economy. In the absence of any other major initiatives this de-rating scheme, plus Chamberlain's reorganisation of local government, formed the backbone of the Conservatives' re-election platform. But the scheme did not have the dramatic effects Churchill had anticipated and few people were impressed enough with it to vote Conservative.

What Churchill was up against was an economy facing fundamental change. The traditional industries (such as coal and steel) were in decline, fighting cheaper imports, and new industries faced the uncertainties of an unstable world economy. And he was straitjacketed not only by the insistence that the country not go further into debt, or increase public spending, but by the refusal to contemplate protectionist policies. Since their defeat at the polls in 1923, when they had promoted tariff reform, the Conservative Party had retreated from this position to support instead the continuance of free trade. During his Chancellorship Churchill did introduce a small number of duties, on silk, wine and sugar, for example, but he also reduced or abolished some, such as those on tea and dried fruits. Thus prevented from being able to raise significant income from import duties, Churchill had a limited range of options. 'With hindsight, Churchill's Chancellorship can be seen as a final, spirited attempt to revive the political economy of 1914 before it was overwhelmed in the Slump.'[5]

A return to 1914 proved impossible, of course. Taxation was no longer high enough to cover government spending. Pre-war budgets of £197 million were unrealistically low, given the increased national debt and cost of social benefits for the unemployed, retired and sick. Eight hundred million pounds proved to be a much more realistic sum for budgets of the inter-war years. Churchill's own lack of expertise in finance probably contributed to the failure to experiment, but the overall consensus was of financial conservatism. To overcome this Churchill needed an expertise and confidence in finance that he simply did not possess.

What he did have was a commitment to social reform. Now that he was Chancellor, he aimed to make the Treasury 'an active instrument of Government social policy'[6] by increasing spending on pensions, social benefits and housing. The main domestic legislation of Baldwin's government was in social reform, taking up some of the themes of the pre-war Liberal administrations. Churchill felt comfortable financing social reform, so that – unusually – the relationship between the Treasury and Neville Chamberlain's Ministry of Health was a cooperative one. As a result, several important schemes were implemented: the Widows and Old Age Pensions Act of 1925 and the National Health Insurance Act, increasing the number of people eligible for pensions and unemployment benefit. In addition, Churchill's Treasury agreed to finance a fifteen-year scheme to subsidise the construction of houses by local authorities, and Baldwin's government saw a more than fourfold increase in the number of new-build houses. That Chamberlain could work with such a supportive Chancellor meant he was able to implement substantial reform in local government too, which enhanced his reputation more than that of his rival. Churchill's budget of 1928 showed flashes of ingenuity in financing this scheme and his own de-rating proposal through introducing a new tax on petrol.

'[T]o finance these impressive schemes of social welfare meant imposing a rigorous policy of retrenchment elsewhere'[7] so Churchill could not share the political rewards for these achievements. This retrenchment, combined with the inflated value of the pound and an unreadiness to consider Keynesian solutions, meant Churchill's Treasury lacked the resources to tackle the deep-seated problems of an economy in the throes of great structural change. Along with other finance ministers of the time, Churchill failed to comprehend the depth and significance of these changes, and was therefore unable to lift Britain out of the depression. His policies had lacked consistency and had produced mixed results. After the financial crisis of 1931, Churchill himself recognised how out of date his economic ideas and understanding had been. Free trade and the Gold Standard were no longer enough to stabilise Britain's economy. But, as Addison has since written, 'In defence of Churchill it had to be asked whether, in the circumstances, anyone else would have done any better.'[8]

Questions

1. 'The return to the Gold Standard in 1925 was a more significant cause of depression in Britain than the Wall Street Crash in 1929.' To what extent do you agree with this view?
2. What economic problems did Churchill fail to address during his years as Chancellor of the Exchequer?

ANALYSIS (2): TO WHAT EXTENT WERE CHURCHILL'S ACTIONS DURING THE GENERAL STRIKE IN 1926 TYPICAL OF HIS ATTITUDE TOWARDS LABOUR?

Upon the outbreak of the General Strike, Baldwin is reputed to have remarked, 'I'm terrified of what Winston is going to be like.'[9] His reputation for belligerence towards labour protest was well known and was reinforced in many people's minds by his actions and words during the tense days of the General Strike. His colleagues in government, too, condemned his attitude towards the trade unions, but they thought his approach was too conciliatory during the long-running miners' strike. What, then, to make of this contradiction? Churchill's reputation with the labour movement is still poor today, linked as he is with events at Tonypandy in 1910, and the labour problems of the immediate pre-war and post-war years.

Churchill's behaviour during the General Strike showed many similarities with these earlier clashes with labour. 'Churchill's mood was of the utmost bellicosity and, some of his colleagues thought, utmost irresponsibility as well.'[10] He argued that tanks should escort the food convoys into London and that machine-guns be set up at key points along the routes to counter any attack. He also advocated a government takeover of the BBC, to broadcast state propaganda. These seemed extreme to other Cabinet ministers, who feared he was spiralling out of control. As the historian Addison admits, 'he was all for heightening the conflict. Needless to say he did not intend to risk a bloody civil war. But he wanted to shake an intimidating fist at the strikers.'[11] Baldwin successfully diverted Churchill's energies into running the *British Gazette*, the government's emergency newspaper. He proved ideally suited to filling the information gap left by the national strikes.

What his colleagues found so disturbing about Churchill's reaction to the strike was his apparently instinctive recourse to militaristic action. Another of his biographers, Norman Rose, has stated: 'in principle, he was not different from the rest of his Cabinet colleagues. What separated them was his style and manner of behaviour.'[12] Most of the Cabinet believed as he did that the General Strike was a constitutional challenge to the government. Where perhaps he differed was in believing it to be 'a dramatic and conscious challenge to the constitution',[13] and that he therefore saw his behaviour during the strike 'as a continuation of his crusade against Bolshevism'.[14]

He had never viewed socialism with anything but extreme suspicion. After the Bolshevik Revolution in 1917 he grew to fear it, too. Indeed the Bolsheviks had committed themselves to exporting socialist revolution abroad, something they appeared nearly to succeed at during 1920, when at war with Poland. Churchill believed 'this band of cosmopolitan conspirators are aiming to constantly overthrow all civilised countries'[15] and as an aristocratic, paternalistic politician, he could imagine nothing worse than the destruction of the existing social order. Carlton has argued that Churchill believed the whole labour movement – trade unions and the Labour Party alike – 'had been dangerously infected with the Bolshevik virus'.[16] He had information that the Comintern (the Soviet body for exporting revolution abroad) had been sending money to British strikers since early 1926. This just reinforced his fear that Bolsheviks were plotting revolution in Britain, and that the General Strike was part of the plot. He could recall the narrowly averted national railway strike of 1911, when he had had information of German support for the strikers. Unlike his colleagues in 1926, he had personal experience of this episode. Then, too, he had amassed troops. When the threat of national action was over, he came to believe that his threat to use the military had forced the unions to back down. In 1926 he was merely repeating this tactic, but this time, surrounded by the moderates of Baldwin's Cabinet, his tactics looked even more extreme. The episode 'exposed in Churchill the lack of steady English restraint for which he had so often been criticised'[17] but for which his colleagues were renowned.

However, the industrial turmoils of 1911 or 1926 were in themselves extreme. When faced by more typical strike action, Churchill's reaction was neither militant nor confrontational. His attempts to find a fair solution to the miners' dispute of 1925–1926 stand out as a 'sustained pacific effort'.[18] His efforts were thwarted in the end not by the unions or miners, but by the mine owners and later by his own colleagues. Both owners and ministers rejected his suggestion that the miners' wage settlement be based on a national minimum wage because they believed it conceded too much to the strikers. Churchill's proposal that a Royal Commission investigate the state of the coal industry in 1925, his agreement to pay a subsidy to the industry to tide it over until the Commission could report, and his attempts to reach a compromise in the summer of 1926 reveal his determination to find a fair, not punitive, settlement for the miners.

He made a clear distinction between the miners' strike, which he saw as being based in genuine grievances, and the General Strike that to him was a purely political act. This distinction is what formed Churchill's opinion that the former required a fair hearing and solution while the latter had to be met by force if necessary. This had been the case sixteen years earlier at Tonypandy. It was Churchill's hesitation over the use of troops that had led to the deaths there, not that he had deployed them in expectation of bloodshed. Here is Churchill's conviction that the trade unions should be separated from politics. It was what he most distrusted about the Labour Party, that its finances, authority and policies were all rooted in trade unions that he suspected of being infiltrated by Bolshevism.

There were in fact few such extremists in either the Labour Party or British trade unions, but he remained convinced that if Labour should come to power chaos would ensue. He abandoned the Liberal Party in 1923 because he was infuriated by the decision to support Labour, enabling the latter to form its first government in Britain. During the election campaign of 1924, he leapt upon the 'Zinoviev letter', now recognised as being a probable fake, and 'played the anti-Bolshevik card for all it was worth'.[19] His campaigning revolved around this scare, that the Comintern was urging the British Communist Party to prepare for revolution. More notoriously, he launched vicious attacks on the Labour Party during the election of 1945. He claimed that if Labour were elected, it would have to establish a Gestapo-like organisation in order to govern effectively. This attack was astonishing because Churchill had been sharing power with Labour in the wartime government of 1940–1945, the purpose of which had been to defeat the fascist state of Nazi Germany. It lost Churchill a great deal of respect; even his daughter reprimanded him for poor judgement in making such wild and unsubstantiated allegations.

There had been times when he had been able to work in harmony with both elements of labour – the trade unions and the political party. During the latter half of the 1930s, his rearmament campaign gathered some support from within the labour movement. He spoke at trade union demonstrations in favour of increased military spending, alongside men like Ernest Bevin, against whom he had battled during the General Strike. Indeed, when he came to form his first War Cabinet in May 1940, Churchill recognised the need to retain the loyalty of the workforce and ensured that the post of Minister of Labour was given Cabinet rank. Furthermore, he proposed to the Labour leader Clement Attlee that Bevin, then Secretary of the Transport and General Workers Union, be appointed Minister of Labour. Despite habitual suspicion of each other, they came to recognise each other's talents and, on the whole, to work well together.

Churchill's attitude to labour was, then, complex. It was rooted in the fact that he was a profoundly conservative man. Able to accept that the working classes could have grievances in genuine need of fair resolution, and that it was the responsibility of the ruling class to meet this need, he could never accept that labour had the right to raise a direct challenge to the established social and political order. He knew that that order was undergoing inevitable and radical change, but he could not contemplate that Britain could succumb to anything so drastic as revolution. He was convinced she should manage change as she had in the past, through incremental and constitutional change. He failed to see the differences between the ideologies of the British Labour Party and trade union movement, which was a moderate one under the leadership of men like Walter Citrine, and those of the Bolsheviks in the Soviet Union. He equated them all with the most extreme form of socialist thought. His rejection of socialism meant that he therefore also rejected the Labour Party – until the dire circumstances of 1940 forced him to think otherwise. His offer of alliance to the Soviet Union in the following year was probably the most personally difficult political decision he had to take, since Stalin's Soviet Union embodied the very revolution against which he had fought so strongly.

His actions during the General Strike were typical, then, of his attitude to only one aspect of the labour movement – its ability to raise the spectre of social revolution. And it was typical of his attitude in 1926. This underwent changes that Churchill could not possibly have foreseen in the shattering years of the Second World War.

Questions

1. Was the General Strike of 1926 an 'attempted revolution'?
2. What evidence is there in Churchill's career to 1929 to support the view that he was an enemy of labour and the trade union movement?

SOURCES

1. CHURCHILL'S YEARS AS CHANCELLOR OF THE EXCHEQUER

Source A: extract from 'The Economic Consequences of Mr Churchill', by J. M. Keynes, published in 1925

The prices of our exports in the international market are too high. About this there is no difference of opinion . . . We know as a fact that the value of Sterling money abroad has been raised by 10 per cent, whilst its purchasing power over British labour is unchanged. This alteration in the external value of Sterling money has been the deliberate act of the Government and the Chancellor of the Exchequer, and the present troubles of our export industries are the inevitable and predictable consequences of it.

The policy of improving the foreign-exchange value of Sterling up to its pre-war value in gold from being about 10 per cent below it, means that, whenever we sell anything abroad, either the foreign buyer has to pay 10 per cent *more in his money* or we have to accept 10 per cent *less in our money*. That is to say, we have to reduce our Sterling prices, for coal or iron or shipping freights or whatever it may be, by 10 per cent in order to be on a competitive level. If Mr Churchill had restored gold by fixing the parity lower than the pre-war figure, or if he had waited until our money values were adjusted to the pre-war parity, then these particular arguments would have no force. But on doing what he did in the actual circumstances of last spring, he was just asking for trouble. For he was committing himself to force down money-wages and all money-values, without any idea how it was to be done. Why did he do such a silly thing?

Partly, perhaps, because he has no instinctive judgement to prevent him making mistakes; partly because, lacking this instinctive judgement, he was deafened by the clamorous voices of conventional finance; and most of all, because he was gravely misled by his experts.

Source B: the previous Labour government had also wanted a return to the Gold Standard

Snowden had no quarrel in principle with what Churchill had done. His own policy at the Treasury [while Chancellor for the Labour government] had been to move towards the Gold Standard, and it was a committee selected by him which had made the crucial recommendation. A month earlier he had written an article in the *Observer* calling for a return to gold at the earliest practicable moment. Among the left wing of the Labour Party, however, there was considerable disquiet, based less on reasoned economic analysis than on a simple fear that the whole operation was a banker's ramp, designed to do down the workers.

Source C: Churchill faced continuous pressure to reduce taxation and public spending, as this 1926 letter to *The Times*, from the League to Enforce Public Economy, demonstrates

Sir, – With the opening of a new Session the people have the right to look to Parliament for the long-promised and long-postponed economies in public expenditure, and if they are not forthcoming to demand an account from those responsible. After the losses caused by the strike, it is more than ever necessary that public burdens should be reduced.

It will be remembered also that in 1925 Mr Churchill promised annual reductions of £10,000,000 a year during his term of office. [But] his actual expenditure for the financial year 1925–26 exceeded his Estimates by £26,000,000, and the estimated expenditure of his second Budget was over £824,000,000.

I know that economy is an old-fashioned remedy and that bureaucracy is too strongly entrenched to be easily retrenched. But the Government has been slipping down a dangerous slope, and men of public spirit should combine, regardless of party attachments, in the coming Session of Parliament to restore thrift to public life.

Source D: a historian sums up the consequences of the return to the Gold Standard

The whole story was a remarkable example of a strong not a weak minister . . . reluctantly succumbing . . . to the near unanimous, near irresistible flow of establishment opinion . . . as a result there was committed what is commonly regarded as the greatest mistake of that main Baldwin government, and the responsibility for it came firmly to rest upon Churchill. Keynes, for instance, wrote a pamphlet, . . . 'The Economic Consequences of Mr Churchill'. In a sense this allocation of blame was unfair, but only in a sense . . . [Churchill] wanted his first budget to make a great splash, which it did, and a considerable contribution to the spray was made by the announcement of the return to Gold. Reluctant convert though he had been, he therefore deserved . . . a considerable part of the blame. An irony was that by up-valuing the pound Churchill threw a destructive spanner in the works of Baldwin's industrial policy . . . The worst possible contribution to industrial peace in our time was to make things more difficult for already suffering traditional export trades, cotton, shipbuilding, steel and above all coal, which was precisely what was done by the return to Gold at the pre-war parity.

Source E: cartoon published in the *Daily Mirror*, April 1928

Figure 1 *The Budget and the Taxpayer* © J. Churchill, *Daily Mirror* (strips and cartoons) with acknowledgements. Centre for the Study of Cartoons and Caricature, University of Kent, Canterbury for the print.

Questions

1. Read Source A. Explain Keynes's use of the term 'conventional finance'. (3)
2. In what ways do Sources A and B add to our understanding of how the decision to return to the Gold Standard was made? (5)
3. What evidence is presented in Sources C and E of the pressures that Churchill faced as Chancellor in the years 1924–1929? (5)
4. To what extent do Sources A and D agree on the consequences of the return to the Gold Standard? (5)
5. 'The return to Gold at the pre-war parity made it almost inevitable that Baldwin's desire for "peace in our time" became the General Strike in fourteen months.' How far do you agree with this statement? Use these Sources and your own knowledge in your answer. (12)

Worked answer

3. Source C is a useful piece of contemporary evidence of the pressure Churchill faced from those who believed that government expenditure should be reduced to the extent of reducing the size of the civil service. Following on from the General Strike, and its associated costs, the author of this letter to *The Times* believed that it was an urgent task of Parliament 'to restore thrift to public life'. Churchill's first budget had undertaken to finance the introduction of new pension schemes for widows and orphans, reinforcing the fact that he did not share the Conservative commitment to minimal state spending and was, therefore, an unusual Tory Chancellor. Source E, also contemporary, expresses a similar view, although this focuses on the supposed greed of Churchill for raising more taxes. In portraying Churchill as the murdering barber, Sweeney Todd, who cut up and baked his victims in pies, the cartoon is suggesting that Churchill the Chancellor was not going to stop at asking for more taxes, but perhaps might demand the lives (or, more likely, the livelihoods) of taxpayers themselves. These demands to reduce both government expenditure and taxation, at a time of rising costs and falling exports, were impossible for Churchill to meet in his years as Chancellor.

2. CHURCHILL, LABOUR AND THE TRADE UNIONS

Source F: cartoon published in the *Evening Standard*, 1929

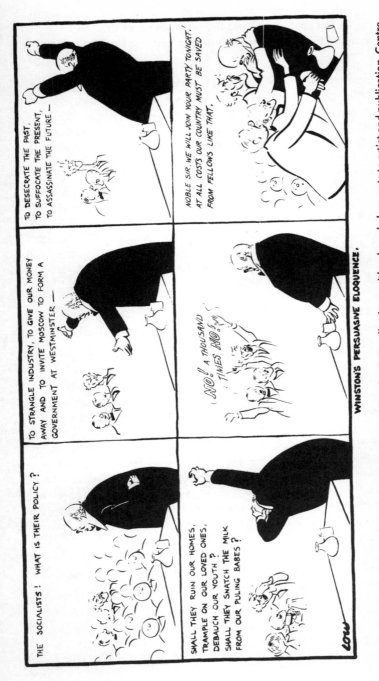

Figure 2 *Winston's persuasive eloquence* © D. Howell, Atlantic Syndications, with acknowledgements to artist and publication. Centre for the Study of Cartoons and Caricature, University of Kent, Canterbury for the print.

Source G: the Labour MP and fierce opponent of Churchill, Emmanuel Shinwell, writing about him in a book published in 1953

Nobody in British politics during the early 'twenties inspired more dislike in Labour circles than Winston Churchill. His crowning sin was the fatuous declaration that Labour was unfit to govern, an accusation that gave the greatest offence to members of the Labour Party. His activities as Chancellor of the Exchequer and as the self-appointed defender of the Constitution during the General Strike served to embitter relations still further between him and the Labour Movement. He was accused of taking decisions that led to a sharp increase in unemployment, of raising state funds in the interests of wealthy taxpayers, and of rejecting attempts to compromise in the General Strike, thus prolonging the dispute. Nor was his conduct as Editor of the official anti-strike paper the *British Gazette* calculated to enhance his reputation among the industrial workers. The mention of his name at Labour gatherings was the signal for derisive cheers; when a Labour speaker found himself short of arguments, he only had to say, 'Down with Churchill.' This never failed to draw thunderous applause.

Source H: in his book *Churchill and the Soviet Union*, David Carlton describes Churchill's reaction to the General Strike

He saw it as a dramatic and conscious challenge to the Constitution and, according to Neville Chamberlain (the Minister of Health), in the days before its commencement was 'getting frantic with excitement and eagerness to begin the battle'. Baldwin put him in charge of the *British Gazette*, remarking privately that 'it will keep him busy, stop him doing worse things' and adding 'I'm terrified of what Winston is going to be like'. In the event the moderate anti-Bolshevik leaders of the TUC rapidly called off the General Strike once they had grasped the constitutional implications. The miners were simply left to face eventual defeat. But Churchill continued to believe that sinister pro-Soviet forces had been seriously involved. It is true of course that the Soviets welcomed the British General Strike and even contributed some funds to assist the strikers and their families. But it seems unlikely that their role in any phase of British interwar industrial relations ... was of any great importance.

Source I: Paul Addison has written about Churchill's actions during, and subsequent reputation after, the General Strike

Ever since the General Strike, tradition has asserted that Churchill played the part of a dangerous extremist, driving the pacific Baldwin into a conflict that might well have ended in bloodshed but for the Prime Minister's skilful control of the fire-eating Chancellor of the Exchequer ... It is quite true that in some ways

Churchill took an extreme line during the strike ... The Cabinet united behind Baldwin's refusal to compromise. Baldwin and the majority worked on the shrewd assumption that the General Council of the TUC could be detached from the miners. They deliberately abstained from language or measures that would drive the 'moderates' of the TUC into a deeper alliance with the 'militants' of the coalfields. Churchill, however, was for piling on the pressure to break the strike. True to form, he was all for heightening the conflict once the issue was joined. Needless to say he did not intend to risk a bloody civil war. But he wanted to shake an intimidating fist at the strikers ... All told, there was much truth in the left-wing notion of Churchill as the extremist of the General Strike. Yet it was convenient for Baldwin, with his carefully constructed reputation as a moderate, that Churchill should be depicted as a menace. Years later [Baldwin] told his biographer, G. M. Young, that the cleverest thing he had ever done was to put Churchill in charge of the *British Gazette*: 'otherwise he would have wanted to shoot someone'. After objections from Churchill, this phrase was deleted from the published version of the biography.

Source J: Norman Rose has also written of Churchill's reactions to the General Strike

Churchill was fully involved in the coal dispute, that had been festering since the end of the war, and that led directly to the great strike. The pre-strike negotiations were prolonged and bitter. Churchill adopted a conciliatory position. He favoured granting a £19 million subsidy – that grew later to £23 million – an offer that blew a hole in his budget but which, together with an intensive enquiry into the ills of the industry, he hoped would preserve industrial peace. This proved to be the basis of a compromise that lasted until the spring of 1926. [But] as the prospect of a fight appeared inevitable, his mood, once conciliatory, turned militant. He was apprehensive lest a pressurized government, bereft of decisive leadership, strike a dishonourable compromise. Once the strike broke out, Churchill's attitude clarified. 'There are two disputes on', he told Baldwin. 'There is the General Strike which is a challenge to the Government and with which we cannot compromise. Strike Notices must be withdrawn unconditionally. There is also a trade dispute in the coal industry: on that we are prepared to take the utmost pains to reach a settlement in the most conciliatory spirit.'

Questions

1. What, according to Source H, was the basis for Churchill's opposition to the General Strike? (3)
2. According to Source J, how did Churchill's attitude differ between the miners' strike and the General Strike? (5)
3. How useful is Source G in understanding Churchill's unpopularity with the Labour Party? (5)

4. To what extent does Source I contradict the assertion that Churchill deserved his reputation as an extremist during the General Strike? (5)
5. Using these Sources and your own knowledge, explain why Churchill opposed the General Strike so vehemently. (12)

Worked answer

1. Source H identifies two reasons for Churchill's opposition to the General Strike: that he saw it as 'a dramatic and conscious challenge to the Constitution', and that he suspected 'sinister pro-Soviet forces' to be sponsoring the strikers.

4

EXILE, 1929–1939

BACKGROUND NARRATIVE

The election result of 1929 was the start of a shift in the political
landscape of Britain, as all the political parties struggled to understand
and interpret the profound changes that had been taking place domes-
tically and internationally since the end of the First World War. The
failure of Baldwin's government to reduce unemployment or to revive
the economy led to its rejection at the polls. With Liberal support,
Ramsay MacDonald formed his second Labour administration.

Although angry at this, Churchill supposed that the Labour government would not last long, based on its brief tenure of office
in 1923–1924. Nor was he concerned at the prospect of being in
opposition for a while. His position as a senior Tory appeared secure,
and he anticipated leading the opposition alongside Baldwin and
Neville Chamberlain, from the front bench. But the issues of India's
status as a dominion and of tariff reform changed these assumptions.
By 1931 Churchill found himself in opposition not just to the Labour
government, but to his own party.

Despite his lifelong adherence to the principles of free trade,
Churchill was forced to accept protectionism by the economic dire
straits of 1931. But he found himself unable to make any such similar
compromise over plans to grant India – the keystone of the British
Empire – dominion status. It was over this issue, therefore, that he

fell out with his party and most of his former colleagues of the 1920s. In following this course of opposition Churchill lost much of the respect he had gained as Chancellor. When the financial crisis forced the formation of the National Government in 1931, Churchill was not even considered for a post in it, despite his wealth of experience. His reputation for confrontation and his record of attacking the Labour Party disqualified him as a suitable member of a cross-party coalition government.

Forced on to the back benches, he remained an energetic MP and public personality. The decade began extremely badly for him personally. He lost a considerable fortune in the Wall Street Crash, and suffered serious injury in a car accident in 1931 from which it took him several months to recover. One of his closest friends (he did not have many), Lord Birkenhead, died in 1930. And his son Randolph, with whom he had a difficult relationship, embarrassed him politically with three unsuccessful attempts to enter Parliament. There were times when Churchill was laid low by bouts of depression, which he referred to as his 'black dog'. He cured himself of this by keeping up a hectic schedule of work – writing books and articles for newspapers and journals, lecturing, appearing in Parliament to lead vigorous political campaigns – and an equally hectic schedule of 'relaxation'. In his spare time, he ran the farm and grounds at his house, Chartwell, in Kent, where he built walls and fed his various animals; he painted, and he entertained on a grand scale. He was not, however, absent from the political stage.

ANALYSIS (1): WHY WAS CHURCHILL SUCH AN ISOLATED FIGURE IN THE PERIOD 1929–1938?

Having completed an unusually long period as Chancellor, Churchill's position on the Tory front bench should have been secure, even after the electoral defeat of 1929. His achievements at the Treasury had admittedly been mixed – but so had those of Baldwin's government as a whole. Defeated at the polls, the Conservative Party lost the self-restraint that had kept the lid on its internal divisions while in government. Churchill had never had much self-restraint. This fault had led him into political controversy and isolation in his earlier career and it was to do so again in this period.

The issue over which he renewed his reputation as a political maverick was the commitment to granting India status as a dominion. Churchill was not the only dissenter; there were others in the party (the 'diehards') and the press (Beaverbrook and Rothermere) who also fought against the Irwin Declaration of 1929 and the subsequent India Bill to reform Indian government. But his objections were more vehemently expressed than those of others, and caught many by surprise. He made no attempt to temper his imperialist views, refusing to retreat from his statements that the loss of India would be an economic disaster for Britain and a political one for India, and persisted with ill-judged 'jibes' about Gandhi. He resigned from the front bench in early 1931, and subsequently campaigned against his own party, and against the tide of majority political thinking on this issue. He fought the passage of the India Bill from its introduction in 1930 until it became law five years later, doing himself 'much harm in the process; he ruled himself out of office for a decade. In the Commons he had become something of a bore'.[1] During the early stages of the campaign, Churchill attracted a substantial amount of support, but his determination to oppose the bill at any cost alienated most of these people, and he lost the chance to build a faction of his own.

Many moderate Conservatives suspected that Churchill was using the India debates to mount a challenge to Baldwin's leadership. Again, Churchill was not alone in being discontented with Baldwin, who was twice on the verge of resigning the leadership, in 1930 and 1931. But there is no evidence to support claims of a Churchill plot to replace Baldwin. His India Defence League was a somewhat improbable selection of people, from eccentric aristocrats to political misfits, with only one issue in common. From the formation of the National Government and its success at the polls in December 1931, Churchill appeared to be the leader of a small and rather extremist splinter group. His challenge for the leadership of the Conservative Party looked highly unlikely to succeed.

His exclusion from the National Government was not only due to his stance over India. It was mostly because his 'colleagues thought that his natural temperament would be antagonistic to the Labour members of a small Cabinet determined to maintain a "national" and united front'.[2] His past record came back to haunt him, from his attacks on the Labour Party during the Zinoviev affair in 1924, the General Strike of 1926 and then MacDonald's Indian policy. Labour had no wish to invite him into Cabinet, but neither, significantly, did any of his past Tory colleagues. They recalled the troubles and discord that his argumentative style had caused in past Cabinets. Men like Baldwin and Chamberlain were probably relieved to be able to exclude him. Chamberlain had not relished his clashes with Churchill during the 1920s, claiming that arguing with Churchill was 'like arguing with a brass band'! The new era of cross-party, consensual government had no room for someone of Churchill's character. Once this new kind of politics had been vindicated by the National Government's victory in the election at the end of 1931, 'Churchill was now clearly superfluous to requirements'.[3]

In other ways too Churchill seemed out of step with the times. He led an aristocratic lifestyle without embarrassment, while Britain suffered the cost of high and rising unemployment. He appeared to flaunt his prejudices with utter disregard for the 'political correctness' of the day, still belonging 'in style and spirit to an age of political adventure which had come to an end . . . He lacked the gentlemanly restraint, and moral respectability of the new regime'.[4] Churchill entered his sixties during this decade. Some felt that his career was at its natural end and that his outbursts over India, Labour and rearmament were the symptoms of an old man's failing judgement. His intervention during the Abdication Crisis of 1936 reinforced these suspicions, as they did suspicions that he was making another bid for the Tory leadership.

Mistrust of his loyalty was never far from the surface, given his history of defections from Tories to Liberals and back again. In stepping into the abdication debate, Churchill claimed to be acting out of personal loyalty to the King, whom he had known since the latter was a boy. 'But the feeling that Churchill was exploiting the crisis for his own ends was strong in both the House of Commons and in the country.'[5] Once again, Churchill misjudged both public and political feeling on this issue, not sharing in the sense of moral outrage that the King should dare to think he could both retain the throne and his position as head of the Church, and marry his divorcee companion, Wallis Simpson. For asking the government to allow more time for the King to come to a decision on his future, Churchill was howled down in the Commons. That he could be so oblivious to the political mood during this episode and in relation to the Indian debates did not bode well for his future in politics. If he had been intending to launch bids for the leadership of the Conservative Party, he had chosen the issues over which to fight spectacularly unsuccessfully. Furthermore, his convictions were completely out of step with those of the majority around him, deepening his isolation.

The Abdication Crisis dashed his hopes of reconciliation with Baldwin's government, just as his campaigning to increase defence spending had begun to attract some favourable attention. From the moment that Hitler came to power in Germany in 1933, Churchill appeared to sense a threat, and to urge greater spending on Britain's air defences. At first he found himself in familiar territory, going against the tide of opinion, which favoured disarmament and spending cuts. His authoritative and persistent claims reaped some reward when, in 1935,

Baldwin offered him membership of the Air Defence Research Subcommittee of the CID (Committee of Imperial Defence). It was an attempt to pacify him rather than bring him into government, though, and despite his obvious experience in military affairs, Churchill continued to be excluded from power. Many observers were amazed that he was not named as the Minister for the Coordination of Defence, a new post created in March 1936.

His continued isolation was sealed when Neville Chamberlain became Prime Minister in May 1937. Churchill himself wrote, 'I had no expectation that he would wish to work with me . . . His ideas were far different from mine on the treatment of the dominant issues of the day.'[6] So while Churchill had hankered after office from 1935, his ambitions were checked again by the promotion of his old rival from the 1920s. By this time Churchill was a consistent critic of the government's policy of appeasing Germany's territorial demands in both the House of Commons and in the many newspaper columns that he authored. Yet it was this policy to which Chamberlain was absolutely committed. Once again Churchill was the advocate of a policy to which the government of the day, and most political opinion, was completely opposed.

Now seen as the reason for his promotion to, and success as, Prime Minister during the Second World War, his outspokenness against appeasement was not popular until the point at which war was imminent. Between 1937 and 1939 the path he trod was lonely and unpopular. Accusations labelling him a warmonger were renewed. It was not until Anthony Eden's resignation as Foreign Secretary in February 1938 that he was joined by a mainstream Tory in his criticisms. As Addison points out, 'the overwhelming majority of Conservatives were enthusiastic supporters of Neville Chamberlain'.[7] Churchill's attacks on appeasement did not, therefore, make people regard him as a prophet; rather he was seen as out of touch with popular and political feelings of dread of another European war. So while 'Churchill's parliamentary attack on Munich made him the central figure . . . in British opposition to Nazism',[8] it did not gain him great support. Indeed, Addison claims that 'his uncompromising denunciation of the Munich agreement resulted in his almost complete isolation in the party during the winter of 1938–9'.[9] During these months Conservative Central Office did its best to foment revolt against him in his own constituency of Epping.

Thus, even during the early months of 1939 Churchill was still in exile, still regarded as leading a misguided, even dangerous, campaign against Chamberlain's foreign policy, and still as the leader of a motley assortment of anti-appeasers who themselves were nothing more than outcasts of the Tory Party.

It was to take an emergency of enormous scale – the outbreak of the Second World War within only twenty-five years of the First – before Churchill's candidacy for ministerial office could be even contemplated. His 'wilderness years' were the price he paid for his past political career. He had consistently broken the rules of ambitious and successful politicians. He had followed a determinedly independent line on almost every political issue, from tariffs to the labour movement, from India to appeasement. It was a habit that was bound to exclude him from the coalitionist administrations of the 1930s. That he chose his issues based on his personal (and unique) set of beliefs, rather than on party lines, meant he never really fitted into a single political party or faction. It was difficult for his contemporaries to find this high level of self-absorption anything but annoying, and usually they found it to be positively repellent. His reputation as an oddity was at the root of his isolation from the political middle ground of this decade.

Questions

1. Was the exclusion of Churchill from the National Governments of 1931–1939 inevitable?
2. Was the Conservative Party Churchill's natural political home?

ANALYSIS (2): 'CHURCHILL'S BELIEF IN THE WHITE MAN'S BURDEN MADE IT IMPOSSIBLE FOR HIM TO ACCEPT THE NOTION THAT INDIA MIGHT ONE DAY BE GOVERNED BY INDIANS.' TO WHAT EXTENT DOES THIS STATEMENT EXPLAIN CHURCHILL'S CAMPAIGN AGAINST INDIAN REFORM IN THIS PERIOD?

It is perhaps surprising that India became such an important issue to Churchill in the early 1930s, since, as a young man, he had regarded his being stationed there as something of a chore. However, his time there between 1896 and 1899 had a lasting influence. It was there that he began to educate himself in history, economics and politics, indulged his love of polo, began to write, and acquired a lifelong taste for whisky.

More seriously, his life there led him to 'the keenest realization of the great work which England was doing in India and of her high mission to rule these primitive but agreeable races for their welfare and our own'.[10] This was written and published by Churchill just as the debate over India was at its height, and as he reflected on this, Churchill acknowledged that he was the product of the Victorian era, when 'the greatness of the

Empire and the duty to preserve it was axiomatic'.[11] This was the crux of the 'white man's burden' in India: 'to reduce to order, to civilise and develop the Native governments we find there'.[12]

Churchill certainly shared this assumption that the British government was superior to that of any Indian prince, and that British rule in India had rescued its peoples from chaotic and dangerous times. He sincerely believed that to retreat from India would reduce it 'to the deepest depths of Oriental tyranny and despotism',[13] that 'the old hatreds between the Moslems and the Hindus [would] revive and acquire new life and malignancy',[14] and 'that measureless disasters would come upon the Indian peoples'.[15] The comment in the title of this question appears, then, to be fair. Churchill did not believe India to be capable of governing herself, as proposed by the India Bill, since her peoples were not yet civilised enough.

He did not, however, believe that Indians would never be able to govern themselves. He had supported the recommendations of the Simon Commission, made in June 1930, that provincial self-government be conceded to India, as a first step towards full independence. What he would not accept was the later proposal for an all-India federation and assembly. A lack of political sophistication, and communal strife between Muslims and Hindus, he argued, would make such a government inoperable.

As well as the damage to Indian peoples Churchill was equally adamant that there would be dire consequences for Britain. British commerce with India was substantial, and he was not the only politician to be concerned at the effects of Indian reform on trade. In particular there were fears for the future of the cotton industry in Lancashire, and that the cost of basic imports from India would rise. In his most colourful speeches Churchill went so far as to predict economic ruin and famine for Lancashire. Such predictions may sound extreme today, but in the world of 1929–1931, economic ruin did not seem so improbable.

Confidence in the international system of finance – from Wall Street to the Bank of England – was repeatedly shattered during these few years. Britain's own financial disaster, in 1931, confirmed for Churchill that the foundations of Britain's power and influence were being irretrievably eroded. For him those foundations consisted of Britain's status as the centre of international finance, the superiority of her navy, and her command of the largest empire in the world. He himself had failed to restore Britain to financial pre-eminence when Chancellor of the Exchequer from 1924–1929, and the Royal Navy had shrunk as a result of spending cuts that he had enforced.

Thus Baldwin's support of the Labour government's intention to grant

India dominion status was viewed by Churchill as an attack on Britain's very status as a world power. He lamented that the British were 'losing their self-confidence in their imperial mission'.[16] He believed this was disastrous for Britain at a time when 'a renewed period of nationalism had begun, in which the great powers were competing for survival'. Instead of retreating, 'what Britain required was a much more robust imperial and foreign policy'.[17] The tenacity with which he conducted the campaign against reform for India was thus inspired as much by concern for Britain's future as a great power as by a conviction that India was not capable of governing itself.

But the passion with which he fought this battle – and many contemporaries thought him consumed by it to the point of obsession – also stemmed from his sense of perplexity and fear of the world situation in which he found himself. The historian Peter Clarke has argued that 'his wild attempt to save the British Raj . . . was symptomatic of his disorientation in a world where the pillars were tumbling'.[18] He confessed to feeling that his political training and experience were no longer relevant to the world he saw before him. He harboured suspicions that the introduction of universal suffrage and the subsequent broadening of democracy had contributed to Britain's decline, by diluting the power of politicians to pursue policies that were unashamedly patriotic and ambitious. During this period he was researching and writing his four-volume biography of the Duke of Marlborough, and looked back at the statesmen and adventurer soldiers of Britain's past with admiration. As he aged – he was fifty-five in 1929 – 'his politics were overlaid by a nostalgia for the past'.[19] His reluctance to admit that India's status had to change was part of this nostalgic regard for the past. Thus his fondness for the achievements of the British Empire and his strong objection to seeing it broken up.

The rhetoric he used in denouncing the plans for India's new status was controversial, and lent credibility to the view that he was an old-fashioned imperialist at heart. He insulted Gandhi by referring to him as a 'half naked fakir' and refused to meet him when he was in Britain for the Round Table Talks in 1931. He was also guilty of making tasteless 'jokes' about him. He was not the only Conservative politician to dislike Gandhi – Chamberlain also was disdainful of him – but Churchill made his comments much more publicly, insensitive to the disapproval this gained him.

Because he campaigned so vociferously and with such application, it was suspected 'that Churchill was only using the India issue to rally the right wing of the Conservative Party so as to replace Baldwin as leader'.[20] Until March 1931 it seemed possible that Churchill might have succeeded. Baldwin's position as party leader was precarious enough, with the party's electoral defeat and internal wrangling over the issue of protectionism threatening to split it. That he decided to support Labour's India policy without consulting the party at all did not improve his popularity. In speaking out against Indian reform, Churchill had the support of almost half of the Conservative MPs. Leading members of his India Defence League included 'scions of three of Britain's greatest aristocratic political families',[21] the Cecils, Cavendishes and Churchills, while the government's rival Union of Britain and India failed to attract any such famous personalities. The IDL was given financial support by the Duke of Westminster, and editorial support by the two dominant press barons of the time, Beaverbrook (whose *Daily Express* was the most popular newspaper then) and Rothermere.

By February 1931 the campaign was going so well it was anticipated Baldwin would soon be forced to resign. Churchill hoped to replace him, and to displace Neville Chamberlain in the process. He considered the possibility of creating a new political grouping, talking with old coalitionists like Austen Chamberlain and Lloyd George, giving substance to those who believed he was actively plotting against Baldwin's leadership. The critical moment came at the beginning of March, when Baldwin came within a hair's breadth of resigning before deciding instead to carry on. He survived – just – and Churchill's opportunity to grasp power was gone. But he 'did not sense the turn of the tide: buoyed by the widespread support he was receiving over India, he marched steadily into a historical cul-de-sac'.[22] It seemed that he had picked the wrong issue over which to try to bring down Baldwin, yet he continued to oppose the reform right until it became law in 1935, well beyond the point at which there was any political gain to be had.

However, there is very little evidence that Churchill saw his stand over India as a bid for the Tory leadership. Rather, it was borne out of personal conviction and not political ambition. Indeed, for such an ambitious politician as Churchill it seems incredible that he remained loyal to his convictions for so long – desperately unpopular as they were to the majority. However, it was important enough for him to lose not only political influence and any chance of occupying the middle ground in the Conservative Party but several friends. It is easy to try to dismiss this episode as an aberration, especially since his views would be politically unacceptable today, but from it came three points of historical significance.

The first, as Stewart argues, was that the threat posed by Churchill's Indian campaign to the stability of the government was serious enough to have its senior members 'running scared'. Rather than being able to ignore him, his activities made them understand what a formidable influence he could be, and to keep an eye on him. Baldwin offered him a seat on the Air Defence Research Committee within only five months of the passage of the India Bill into law. In doing so, he acknowledged Churchill's potential for disruption. He was unwilling to give him any greater role for fear of the power Churchill commanded when he had an issue to champion. This was the second important outcome of the Indian campaign. His obstinacy and the defiance with which he had stuck to his convictions were characteristics to fear and admire. They were qualities required in a crisis of the severity that eventually faced Britain in 1940. The third consequence was Churchill's alienation from the political centre. Campaigning against the India Bill identified him as an anachronistic 'diehard', which was a reputation that was hard for him to shake off, and accounts for the reluctance with which many were prepared to take seriously his statements about Nazi Germany.

In campaigning against Indian reform he exposed his old-fashioned Victorian views on the responsibility of empire, and on the 'primitive' nature of the Indian population. In doing so, he alienated himself from the left wing and moderate elements of the House of Commons, who grew to associate him with opinions that were obsolete. In his India campaign he showed he was a politician who was at the height of his powers when confronted with an issue that threatened to destroy his deeply held principles. In India he found an issue that few others felt as deeply as he did. In appeasement and the rearmament of Germany, he found something altogether different. The question remained whether he would be able to persuade others to listen to, and trust, his next campaign.

Questions

1. How successfully did British governments handle relations with India in the period 1931–1939?
2. In what ways did Churchill's attitude towards India differ from his attitude to other colonies?

SOURCES

1. WHY WAS CHURCHILL SUCH AN ISOLATED FIGURE IN THE 1930s?

Source A: extract from *Churchill*, by Robert Blake, published in 1998

He was not unduly disturbed by loss of office in 1929 and set off with his brother and his son Randolph on an enjoyable tour of Canada and the United States. Back in England, restless and frustrated, though busily writing, he took up a new cause that was to be politically disastrous and keep him out of office for ten 'wilderness years'. This was India. He bitterly objected to Baldwin's agreement to support a bi-partisan policy of limited self-government. He used every trick of parliamentary procedure to block it. He had the support of a die-hard right-wing group of Tory MPs, but the vast majority supported the MacDonald–Baldwin partnership as did the rump of the Labour Party. He failed and did himself much harm in the process; he ruled himself out of office for a decade. In the Commons he had become something of a bore. This was unfortunate, for the next cause that he took up was, unlike India, one that really mattered – the rising threat of Hitler. If he had talked less about India he might have commanded more attention about Germany. His well-justified warnings in the 1930s about German rearmament and British deficiency fell on deaf ears and empty green benches.

Source B: extract from *Burying Caesar: Churchill, Chamberlain and the Battle for the Tory Party* by G. Stewart, published in 1999

The new Government may have been in part constituted to save the very device that Churchill had been responsible for restoring – the gold standard – but his eclipse on economic questions by Chamberlain and his concentration upon the Indian Question came at a time when economy was much more important than events in the subcontinent . . . the fact that the National Government was not formed with the intention of lasting long enough to address the Indian agitation conclusively also undermines the established view on the subject that it was Churchill's India diehardism which kept him out of the Cabinet in August 1931 . . . he was excluded [because] . . . Churchill's colleagues thought that his natural temperament would be antagonistic to the Labour members in a small Cabinet determined to maintain a 'national' and united front . . . India was the most pressing of Churchill's supposedly objectionable right-wing views, but his renowned and age-old combativeness towards the Labour Movement stood to disqualify him from office even if he had waxed lyrical about Indian constitutional reform.

Source C: extract from *Churchill on the Home Front* by Paul Addison, published in 1992

Churchill's antagonism to the policies of MacDonald, Baldwin and Chamberlain arose from the conviction that Britain was a great power in decline . . . In part, Churchill attributed Britain's decline as a great power to the advance of democracy and the introduction of a universal franchise. [He believed that] the most important event apart from the Great War had been the emancipation of women, and their assumption of full citizenship . . . Britain had abandoned the masculine democracy since 1928 . . . [He] feared that women would be too preoccupied with hearth and home to sustain the politics of Empire. Churchill kept up his constitutional arguments for some time. Some observers alleged that his views betrayed fascist tendencies, a suspicion aroused perhaps by his praise of Mussolini . . . in 1933 as 'the greatest law-giver among living men'. Apart from universal suffrage, Churchill blamed the intelligentsia for undermining national self-confidence. On 9 February 1933, ten days after Hitler became Chancellor of Germany, the Oxford Union Debating Society carried by 275 votes to 153 the motion 'that this House will in no circumstances fight for its King and Country'. Churchill was shocked and condemned the resolution as an 'abject, squalid, shameless avowal'.

Source D: cartoon, published in the *Daily Express* on 22 November 1935

VISITOR. "WILL YOU ASK MR. JUMBO BALDWIN IF I CAN JOIN HIS CABINET PARTY? DO YOU THINK HE'LL REMEMBER ME?"
BUTLER. "HELEPHANTS NEVER FORGET, SIR."

Figure 3 This cartoon first appeared in the *Daily Express*, 22 November 1935. Acknowledgements to the artist, Strube, and publisher for permission, © Adam Williams, Express Newspaper plc. Centre for the Study of Cartoons and Caricature, University of Kent, Canterbury for the print.

Source E: cartoon, published in the *Daily Herald* on 30 March 1933

[See opposite]

Nazi Movement—Local Version

Questions

1. Look at Source E: explain the significance of the date of publication of this cartoon. (3)
2. Why, according to the author of Source B, did Churchill fall out of political favour? (5)
3. Look at Sources A and D: to what extent do these two Sources offer different explanations for Churchill's fall from political favour? (5)
4. Of Sources B and D, which is the most reliable evidence of Churchill's political isolation? Give reasons for your answer. (5)
5. 'In 1935 Churchill seemed a man without a future.' Discuss this statement, using evidence from these Sources and your own knowledge. (12)

Worked answer

5. All of these Sources offer evidence to explain Churchill's political decline in the 1930s. The issue that won him the most notoriety was his stand against the India Bill. For Blake (Source A), this opposition was what 'ruled him out of office for a decade', and Strube's cartoon (Source D) reinforces this interpretation. It suggests that even after the passage of the India Act, and a general election, Baldwin (the 'Helephant') refused to forget Churchill's opposition, so excluding him from office. However, Stewart argues in Source B that Churchill was excluded because of his 'antagonistic' behaviour towards the Labour Party. The National Government of 1931 had to build unity, and there was no room for someone like Churchill, with his reputation for being divisive, in a small Cabinet. In Source C Addison describes Churchill's old-fashioned and reactionary views: imperialism, distrust of the female vote and dismissiveness of youthful pacifism. Consequently he was seen by some as having 'fascist tendencies', as Source E illustrates. By 1935 Churchill was sixty-one years old, had had a long political career, and now appeared to be out of step with political and popular cultures. He was also without a political home, with Labourites, Liberals and Conservatives all unable to identify with his views, and it may have seemed probable, even desirable, that he would soon retire.

However, there were other issues on which Churchill spoke, which are not represented in this selection of Sources. He made his first speech against disarmament in early 1932, warning of the threat it posed to European peace, and predicting another war if disarmament was not stopped. Once Hitler became Chancellor, Churchill lost no time in warning that his ambitions boded ill for European peace. His pleas for increased defence spending (especially on aerial defence) took on greater urgency in 1935, with Hitler's declaration that the Luftwaffe had achieved parity with the RAF. In this context Churchill could only despair of the infamous outcome of the Oxford Union debate (Source C). All that remained to be seen was whether Churchill could resurrect his chances, and build a political future through his speeches against disarmament and Germany. In 1935 this must have seemed a slim chance.

2. CHURCHILL'S CAMPAIGN AGAINST APPEASEMENT

Source F: extract from Churchill's speech during the Munich debate in the House of Commons, October 1938

I find unendurable the sense of our country falling into the power, into the orbit and influence of Nazi Germany, and of our existence becoming dependent upon their goodwill or pleasure. It is to prevent that that I have tried my best to urge the maintenance of every bulwark of defence – first, the timely creation of an Air Force superior to anything within striking distance of our shores; secondly, the gathering together of the collective strength of many nations; and, thirdly, the making of alliances and military conventions, all within the Covenant, in order to gather together forces at any rate to restrain the onward movement of this power. It has all been in vain. Every position has been successfully undermined and abandoned on specious and plausible excuses.

Source G: extract from Hitler's speech of 9 October 1938

We are to-day a people of power and strength such as Germany has never known before. However, experience must strengthen our resolution to be careful and never omit anything that should be done to protect the Reich. We have, on the other side, statesmen who, we believe, also want peace. But they rule countries whose inner situation makes it possible for them to be replaced by others who do not want peace – and these others exist. If Churchill came to power in Great Britain instead of Chamberlain we know it would be the aim to unleash immediately a world war against Germany. He makes no secret of it.

Source H: cartoon, published in *Punch* on 2 November 1938

[see p. 66]

Source I: Emmanuel Shinwell, Labour MP and fierce opponent of Churchill, writes about him

And then [in 1938] began that memorable series of speeches by Churchill where the case for rearmament was argued with a skill, lucidity and earnestness which, if it failed to convince the Labour benches, at least earned for the orator the admiration his qualities deserved. Among the Tories his advocacy of more adequate defence preparations, far from gaining unqualified support, created considerable confusion. Bitter exchanges ensued between Baldwin and his former Chancellor of the Exchequer, while on the benches immediately behind Churchill sat a group of Tories who persistently interjected, treating his remarks with derision. It is no exaggeration to say that, while the Labour Party vehemently opposed him, they were more conscious of his gifts than many of his own side of the house. Here was

A FAMILY VISIT

"It was a great work, and I wish you could now add another chapter to your own career."

this striking figure in our political life, this sparkling orator who had held the highest offices in the State, who presented his case with unquestionable sincerity, however misguided we regarded it – scorned by his former colleagues ... most of whom were political midgets in comparison. How could Baldwin ignore Churchill's capabilities in the sphere of defence by appointing Sir Thomas Inskip as the Minister for the Coordination of Defence, who yielded nothing but a weary collection of turgid utterances in our debates, and bored the House to such a degree that hardly anybody could be induced to stay and listen to him?

Source J: extract from *Churchill on the Home Front* by Paul Addison, published in 1992

The overwhelming majority of Conservatives were enthusiastic supporters of Neville Chamberlain. The little band of anti-appeasers looked to Eden as their leader, and were careful not to associate themselves too closely with Churchill. Churchill was too great a rebel, and his policies too unpopular, for the party to stomach. His uncompromising denunciation of the Munich agreement resulted in his almost complete isolation in the party during the winter of 1938–9 ... This was the true period of exile in the wilderness, when Churchill was almost forced to break with his party, ... [but] the pendulum began to swing back in Churchill's favour in March 1939, when Hitler's troops marched into the rest of Czechoslovakia. Churchill grew in stature as his critique of appeasement was vindicated by events – or at any rate appeared to be.

Questions

1. Identify the elements of Churchill's alternatives to appeasement, as described in Source F. (3)
2. Read Sources I and J. To what extent do they agree in their interpretation of Churchill's political reputation? (5)
3. What do Sources G and H add to our understanding of Churchill's political profile at this time? (5)
4. By what point was Churchill identified as the main opponent to appeasement? Use these Sources and your own knowledge to explain your answer. (5)
5. How important was Churchill's opposition to appeasement to his inclusion in the War Cabinet in September 1939? Use your own knowledge and these Sources in your answer. (12)

Worked answer

5. Having established himself as the prime opponent of appeasement in the autumn of 1939, Churchill was able to reap the benefits of the turn against that policy which followed the Nazi annexation of Czechoslovakia in March 1939. The fact that his earlier warnings of Hitler's ambition, and of the inevitable failure of appeasement to satisfy that ambition, began to be proved correct and gave him a reputation as a prophet. Source I is important in the evidence it provides of Churchill's skills as an orator and his consequent persuasiveness for his case. However, it also points to his experience and knowledge of military matters as being superior to anyone in the government, including the Minister for the Coordination of Defence, and his military experience was a vital reason for his inclusion

in the Cabinet in 1939. No other Cabinet member had comparable experience – a considerable liability for a country about to declare war. It was also a Cabinet that had begun to lose its credibility. Its commitment to appeasement had involved Britain in the indefensible sacrifice of an entire country (Czechoslovakia) in a vain hope that war could be avoided. Churchill had played no part in that policy and so was untainted by it. His inclusion in the Cabinet was a way of bolstering its reputation, since he had been identified by Hitler himself as an arch enemy (Source G). Churchill's aggressive tones and calls for rearmament, only recently dismissed as warmongering, suddenly appealed to both the Cabinet and the public. Now on the verge of war, this was the kind of attitude that the government would need if Britain was going to have to fight. Thus his opposition to disarmament was another important reason for his acceptance into Chamberlain's Cabinet. Without these other elements – his military experience, his ability to inspire, his fearless attitude to Germany and his tenacity while in political isolation – all qualified him for inclusion in the War Cabinet. There were other opponents of appeasement – notably Anthony Eden – who were not immediately included, and so it must be concluded that Churchill's inclusion was based upon more than just his condemnation of that policy.

5

FINEST HOUR

BACKGROUND NARRATIVE

In the same way that he dominated the war years, Churchill's history of the Second World War has shaped the way that British histories of the war have been written ever since. His volume dealing with 1940 is entitled 'Their Finest Hour', and it is surely a year about which there is most legend, nostalgia and myth in Britain. This chapter will examine some of those legends.

Churchill's standing was strong at the beginning of the year. As First Lord of the Admiralty, he represented Britain's only world-class service, and the only one that was actively engaged during the so-called 'Phoney War'. News of the navy's victory at the Battle of the River Plate, with the sinking of the German battleship *Graf Spee* in December 1939, had raised his profile with the public. This was followed by another success: a daring rescue of nearly three hundred British prisoners-of-war from the German ship *Altmark*. Churchill took great care to announce these successes personally and so became associated with news of military victory. Chamberlain suffered in comparison. He had declared war very reluctantly and his leadership during the first few months was lacklustre. Moreover, the only member of his Cabinet with any charisma was Churchill. Many of his colleagues were political nonentities. Chamberlain's leadership and regime were ripe, then, to be challenged. But the challenge did not come from Churchill.

It was the failure of the Norway campaign that led to the Prime Minister's downfall, and to the chain of events that replaced him with Churchill. The aim of the invasion plan had been to cut off supplies of Swedish iron ore that were being shipped to Germany through neutral Norwegian waters. The plan was controversial from the start since it involved an attack on a neutral country. But it was also full of risk because it was a combined attack involving all three of the services, they were ill prepared, ill equipped and Norway was still in the depths of winter weather. Churchill had been part of the planning of what he himself called 'this ramshackle campaign', and a supporter of it. Yet when it became clear that it was obviously failing, it was not him who was blamed. When Parliament gathered to debate the campaign on 7 and 8 May 1940 MPs were quick to focus their criticism on Chamberlain's leadership instead.

ANALYSIS (1): HOW AND WHY DID CHURCHILL BECOME PRIME MINISTER IN 1940?

Churchill did not become Prime Minister by winning a general election, or even by winning the support of the majority of his own party. Circumstances in May 1940 were out of the ordinary, to say the least: Britain was at war, and therefore could not afford to be, or appear to be, distracted by an internal political crisis. Therefore, once it had become obvious that Chamberlain had lost the confidence of the House of Commons during the Norway debate of May 1940, there could be no delay in choosing his successor. Churchill's ascent to Prime Ministerial office took place in a whirlwind four days, during which time five major events played key roles in the fall of Chamberlain and the rise of Churchill. An examination of these five events will explain how the careers of these two men changed so dramatically in such a short space of time, and how the outcome was not as inevitable as it may seem today.

The first key event was the two-day parliamentary debate about the Norwegian campaign, which took place on 7 and 8 May 1940, to be followed by an adjournment of the Commons. There was no doubt that the Norwegian campaign had been a failure. Churchill as First Lord of the Admiralty had planned the naval aspects of the campaign months earlier, as an attempt to cut off the shipment of supplies of iron ore from Sweden via Norwegian waters. His plan had been rejected several times until Chamberlain suddenly reversed his decision and approved it in late March. By this time it was too late. Only days after the British began their campaign Hitler's forces invaded Denmark and Norway, quickly establishing superiority in the air. This, and the failure of the British to coordinate between their army and navy led to defeat and evacuation from Norway.

This dismal news was the backdrop to 'one of *the* classic parliamentary occasions of the twentieth century'.[1] 'On 7–8 May the House convened, ostensibly to debate the Norwegian campaign, but in fact to review the government's overall war record.'[2] The first day's debate went badly for Chamberlain, as a growing number of MPs stood up to criticise both the military actions and domestic policies of his wartime administration. The most devastating attacks came from Sir Roger Keyes, whose speech was all the more powerful for the fact that he wore his admiral's uniform and six rows of medals, and from Leo Amery. The latter had been a colleague and supporter of Chamberlain, so it came as a shock that his speech not only was critical but asked him to consider resigning. Chamberlain was visibly shaken and by the end of the first day it was clear he was seriously wounded.

However, few believed that he would be forced to resign. He led the Conservative Party with a huge majority in the Commons. And there was no consensus on who could take his place as Prime Minister. There were a number of Tory rebel groups, which each held different views about the government's and Chamberlain's future. Even the Labour opposition had not planned Chamberlain's downfall. 'There was nothing artificial or choreographed about the pattern the debate took'[3] over the two days. Labour and the Tory rebels did not coordinate their opposition during the debate, even though they often shared common ground in the criticisms they made of Chamberlain's administration. And it was not until Labour had seen the extent of discontent within the Conservatives that they finally 'scented blood' and decided to force a division of the House. On the second day, Herbert Morrison announced Labour's decision to vote against the proposed adjournment. This was a way of forcing a vote of no confidence in Chamberlain, since it would give all MPs the chance to use their vote as an expression of their discontent in, or support for, his government. Morrison's announcement brought into the open the fact that the debate had been less about Norway and much more about Chamberlain's record as wartime leader.

The second day was dominated by acrimonious and sometimes personal attacks on Chamberlain. Churchill's vigorous closing speech was good but not good enough to save the day. The votes came back: 281 for and 200 against. It was a victory for the government but an empty one. Its majority of over 200 had fallen to only 81 votes. Over forty Tories had voted against their own party and forty had abstained. There was pandemonium in the Commons as Chamberlain stalked out amid shouts for him to resign.

What had inspired such dissatisfaction? Having been reluctant to go to war, Chamberlain had been just as reluctant to organise the kind of war effort that could sustain Britain through another world war. A man whose 'mind ran on rails' proved ill suited to adapting to a war that had broken all the rules. The Norway campaign had symbolised this. Having appointed not Churchill (who was best qualified) but Chatfield as Minister for the Coordination of Defence, military planning lacked that very thing – coordination. So Chamberlain created a Military Coordination Committee, but this merely added another layer of bureaucracy and slowed down the decision-making process. By the time he had given greater authority to Churchill it was too little and too late. Frustrated with the situation, Churchill drove the Chiefs of Staff to the brink of mutiny. This system 'came near to collapse during the Norwegian campaign'.[4]

This failure of military planning was a significant one for Chamberlain. Sixteen of those Conservatives who voted against him at the end of the Norway debate were serving in the forces. They had other concerns, too. There was a growing sense of alarm at how ill equipped the army was; there was a shortage of almost every kind of military necessity, from uniforms to ammunition. At the root of these shortages was another failure of organisation and coordination. Addison has written that, 'the major criticism of Chamberlain centred on his refusal to institute stronger coordination of the economy'.[5] Indeed, there were no fewer than six separate government departments operating in economic affairs: the Board of Trade and the Ministries of Labour, Supply, Food, Shipping and Economic Warfare. With two separate coordinating committees it was another example of bureaucracy blocking any chance of progress.

As a result, British industry had been unable to achieve efficient war production. Despite one million unemployed, there was still an acute shortage of skilled workers and many key factories were unable to work at full capacity. This had led to serious bottlenecks in production and to rising wages, neither of which could be afforded while at war. Labour, trade unions and ministers had all pointed out these problems. Churchill argued that the failure to organise the labour force meant that the vital motor and aircraft manufacturing industries and engineering had still not been reorganised on a war production footing by May 1940. Chamberlain's solution had been to appoint Kingsley Wood as chairman of the Cabinet's Home Policy and Food Policy committees in April, but much more drastic action was needed than that. During the Norway debate, many of the speakers expressed their dissatisfaction and concerns with the economic situation. Few believed that Britain could continue to fight unless major changes were made – quickly – to make her economy more efficient.

The debate was also used to express concerns over the politically narrow base of Chamberlain's government and the poor quality of many of his Cabinet ministers. Simon, Chancellor of the Exchequer, and Hoare, Lord Privy Seal, were the most unpopular with the rebels and with Labour. The Cabinet consisted of men who had remained loyal to Chamberlain's policies (with the notable exception of Churchill), but many felt it was time that this be broadened out to include those Tories who had been anti-appeasers, and even to include the leaders of the Labour Party. In particular, the rebel groups within the Conservative Party – the anti-appeasers and the diehards – were growing in their dissatisfaction at their continued exclusion, and in numbers. In 1940 Harold Nicolson had noted in his diary that he felt 'all the more able Conservatives' were with the rebels, and it is revealing to note that two future Conservative Prime Ministers, Eden and Macmillan, were in the rebel camp by this time. However, the rebels were about to stamp their authority on the political scene.

Their meeting on 9 May was the second event leading to Churchill's accession to power. From it they concluded that they would support any Prime Minister who could form a National Government and carry the confidence of the nation. Then they announced this to the press, making it public and so forcing Chamberlain to ask Labour if they would agree to serve under him in a new National Government. He was deeply disliked by Labour and it looked unlikely that he would be able to persuade them to join his Cabinet. Nevertheless, Chamberlain, stubborn to a fault, decided to try. Attlee and Morrison, the Labour leaders, agreed to put the decision to the party's Executive Committee at their national conference about to take place in Bournemouth.

Meanwhile, the third event of great importance in Churchill's rise to power took place at 10 Downing Street that same afternoon, 9 May. He, Halifax, Chamberlain and the Chief Whip, Margesson, met, knowing that a successor had to be chosen, should Chamberlain be unable to form a National Government. Halifax and Churchill were the only possible candidates. Halifax was the favourite of Chamberlain, most of the Conservative Party and the King (the King held the power to appoint the Prime Minister), having had long years of political experience and loyalty in his favour. Against him was that he was strongly associated in the public eye with the now discredited policy of appeasement. Churchill, on the other hand, was also a controversial candidate. He had won much public support and affection while at the Admiralty, having 'asserted himself as the most newsworthy of Chamberlain's Ministers'[6] by managing the announcements of naval battles and successes to his advantage. At this time the Royal Navy was the only force with an active role in the otherwise 'Phoney War'. Thus successes like the sinking of the German battleship *Graf Spee* were instant and welcome news items in an otherwise dreary few months. He was also untainted by an association with appeasement, having campaigned against it since the late 1930s. However, 'the gap between his popular standing and his credibility with Whitehall was considerable'.[7] It was not the public who could choose the next Prime Minister, and there were many MPs and civil servants who dreaded the thought of him holding that office.

In the end the decision was not made by any of these people. Halifax had already decided that he did not want to become Prime Minister, and, when offered the position, turned it down flat. He knew he did not have the right qualities to lead Britain through a long war. He also knew that he would soon be overshadowed by Churchill's superior grasp of military planning. Instead, he, and probably Chamberlain too, thought he would be more effective as a restraining, moderating influence over Churchill, and a safe alternative should Churchill fail. Halifax's refusal was pivotal to Churchill's succession. With no one else to consider, Chamberlain and Margesson had no other choice but Churchill. When the meeting broke up Chamberlain was still hopeful that the Labour Party might agree to serve under him, and that he could form a new National Government and somehow survive as Prime Minister.

But his unpopularity with Labour made this impossible. In the fourth key step towards his political demise and Churchill's rise, Attlee telephoned Chamberlain to inform him of his party's decision that they would not join him in forming a new government. As well as a long history of 'disdain for Labour doctrines',[8] Chamberlain's war record with Labour had been poor. He had refused to recognise that 'Representatives of the workers needed to be directly involved, not only in the shaping of wartime policy, but in the political balance in Parliament.'[9] Without this partnership the economy was not going to be able to sustain a war effort on the huge scale demanded by this war against Germany. Yet Chamberlain had rebuffed most attempts by the trade unions to create such a working partnership. This lack of attention to the problem of reorganising industry and the workforce led many in the Labour Party trade union and movement to 'fear that if the Conservatives were left to run the war, it would end in another terrible slump, with war workers thrown on the scrap heap'.[10] They had lost confidence in Chamberlain as a leader who would be able either to find or implement solutions. Churchill was not their unanimous choice as his successor. His relations with Labour and the trade unions had been difficult, too. But in him they saw someone with the energy, determination and imagination to tackle these problems with the urgency they needed.

The final stage in Churchill's long road to becoming Prime Minister was the War Cabinet meeting on 10 May. Holland and Belgium had just been invaded, and Chamberlain announced to his ministers his intention to stay on – that it was the wrong moment to step down. Kingsley Wood, formerly loyal to Chamberlain, made it plain he thought it was time for him to resign. Having been appointed to the Home and Food Policy committees, he had been dismayed by the extent of Britain's economic problems. At some point during the Norway debate he had decided to switch allegiance from Chamberlain to Churchill. After more persuasion Chamberlain finally resigned and recommended to the King that he send for his rival, Churchill, to ask him to form a new National Government.

'Looking back on the political crisis of May 1940 with the aid of hindsight, we must remark on how uninevitable the "inevitable" seemed to be at the time. Many experienced commentators expected the Chamberlain government to survive.'[11] Few predicted that Churchill could have risen so rapidly, or that events could have led to such an unexpected promotion. Churchill had succeeded Chamberlain by winning over enough Conservative and Labour MPs by proving himself more suited to the demands of wartime leadership. As Churchill wrote in his memoirs, 'I felt as if I were walking with destiny, and that all my past life had been but a preparation for this hour.'[12]

Questions

1. 'It had been frustrating not to be a man of power, but his lack of office was in fact his salvation.' To what extent was Churchill's opposition to appeasement important in his appointment as Prime Minister in 1940?
2. What problems did Churchill face in establishing his authority as Prime Minister, and how did he overcome them?

ANALYSIS (2): WHY DID CHURCHILL AND THE WAR CABINET DECIDE TO FIGHT ON IN MAY 1940?

Churchill laid bare his intent in his first speech as Prime Minister on 13 May: 'Victory at all costs.' It seemed an absurd statement when at that moment the odds against Britain's survival as an independent state were stacked so high. By the end of May, German forces had overrun Holland and Belgium and had breached French defences in only three weeks of fighting. How could Britain hope to defend herself against such military superiority when most of her army was trapped in Belgium?

Churchill's own account of this critical period gives the impression that neither he nor the War Cabinet contemplated anything other than Britain fighting on. In fact, a fierce debate raged between Halifax, who wanted to explore the possibilities for a negotiated peace with Germany, and Churchill, who did not, for a number of days at the end of May 1940. During those few days, Britain's (and Churchill's) fate hung in the balance.

David Reynolds has written that 'the debates about peace in May 1940 turned on gut instinct'.[13] Few people could have been in doubt as to Churchill's gut instinct. His reputation had been built on his outspoken distaste for Hitler's regime. His gut instinct told him that a man who talked in terms of a fight to the death, the extinction of weak races and nations and the supremacy of the German 'master race' was unlikely to allow the survival of an independent Britain and her empire for very long. Thus he was unable to believe that an approach to Hitler, to discover what peace terms he might offer Britain, could produce anything worthwhile.

His Foreign Secretary, Halifax, on the other hand, hoped that an approach to Hitler could save Britain from the likely destruction and humiliation of open conflict with Germany. He proposed to use Mussolini, who was still a neutral in the war in May 1940, as the intermediary between Britain and Germany. The core of his proposal was that 'If Signor Mussolini will co-operate with us in securing a settlement of all the European questions which safeguard the independence and security of the Allies, and could be the basis of a just and durable peace in Europe',[14] Britain should consider meeting Italian demands for territory in the Mediterranean and/or North Africa. If the attempt failed, Halifax argued, Britain would have lost nothing.

Churchill disagreed. For him, 'May 1940 was the very worst moment to show a lack of resolve' since it 'would fuel Hitler's appetite'.[15] Churchill's logic was to ask why, when intoxicated by the speed and ease of his conquests, Hitler would offer fair and reasonable terms to Britain. Surely he would view an approach as a sign of weakness and, as he had done with other countries in similar circumstances since 1938, would take his chance to impose punitive terms and even occupation. Indeed, Churchill 'recognised, as the French discovered, that peace on Hitler's terms would be shortlived and one-sided'.[16] Where Halifax and Chamberlain were willing to gamble on Hitler's willingness to leave Britain in peace, Churchill saw no reason to place trust in a man who had flouted all diplomatic and military norms since 1936. Churchill's gamble was to believe that Britain's people would support his conviction that they had to 'fight on unconquerable until the curse of Hitler is lifted'.[17]

But before persuading the people to fight on, he had to persuade two of his most powerful colleagues, Halifax and Chamberlain, to do so. They, not Churchill, who had been Prime Minister for only a few weeks, held the loyalty of the Conservative Party. Halifax's proposed approach to Mussolini appeared very sensible at this time: Belgium was about to surrender and British and French forces had been cut off by the German advance into France. The War Cabinet debated the issue on 27 and 28 May. The first day went badly for Churchill, with Halifax losing his temper and threatening to resign. Churchill knew that he could not survive if this should happen and walked with his unhappy Foreign Secretary in the garden of Number 10 to calm him down.

But, determined to win the debate, Churchill called a meeting of the wider Cabinet for the following day, 28 May. At this, he subjected his ministers to a forceful and emotional presentation of Britain's situation, ending melodramatically by declaring: 'If this long island history of ours is to end at last, let it end when each one of us lies choking in his own blood upon the ground.'[18] Many of those present were moved to jump up to shake his hand and pledge to fight on. 'It was an unprecedented scene. This, more than any other time, appeared to be the moment when the Prime Minister was walking with destiny.'[19] When Churchill met with the War Cabinet later that same afternoon he knew that he had the support of the outer Cabinet and could outmanoeuvre Chamberlain and Halifax. It had been the pivotal moment of Churchill's government. Had Halifax resigned, Churchill may not have survived. A different leader may have sued for peace with Germany. Certainly Hitler had expected Britain to do so, since his whole strategy depended on her being neutralised, freeing him to concentrate on his war in the east.

So was it right that Churchill 'imposed his vision'[20] on the Cabinet, committing Britain and her empire to a war that was more bloody and lasted much longer than most had been able to imagine in 1940? Revisionist historians have asked whether it was right for Churchill to have believed that Hitler's terms would have been so unacceptable that there was no alternative but to carry on, and to have turned his 'gut instinct' into national policy. But his conviction rested on more than just that. He, along with many experienced observers, believed the German economy to be on the verge of collapse, overstretched by the demands of Blitzkrieg. With hindsight this was a mistaken view, but at the time it seemed incredible that an economy that had been in disarray in the 1920s could now sustain such an intensive war only a decade later.

Churchill was also convinced that the United States would soon enter the war on Britain's side. He had been corresponding with President

Roosevelt since 1939 and believed it possible that he would declare war on Germany once he had been re-elected in November 1940. Calculating that Britain could manufacture or buy enough armaments to hold out until then was a risk, but Churchill took that risk because he had enormous faith in his ability to inspire, bully and organise government and industry into an explosion of increased productivity. Again, his confidence paid off, since Britain produced more aircraft than Germany in 1940, when the most critical air battles (the Battle of Britain and the Blitz) were fought. And while most ministers were pessimistic about the chances of rescuing Britain's forces at Dunkirk from the German advance, Churchill had ordered preparations for a huge evacuation exercise. He had expected only 50,000 men to be rescued, but when he heard that half that number had been rescued in just one day, 28 May, he knew he had been right to insist on fighting on. As more troops were evacuated, Britain stood more chance of rebuilding a reasonable defence force against a possible German invasion. By the end of the evacuation a quarter of a million men had been rescued to fight another day. The effect of this was to raise the spirits of many in Britain who had expected a rout.

Similarly, Churchill had believed that 'the effect on the morale of our people [of seeking peace terms with Hitler] would be extremely dangerous'.[21] He neither consulted the public nor read opinion polls, despite promising to commit the population to a long war of 'blood, toil, tears and sweat'. Yet he understood that talk of peace with Hitler would destroy morale. He had seen at close hand the reactions of the French government and people to the German invasion and drew the conclusion that to talk of capitulation was to make it inevitable. So while Churchill often made his arguments using emotional language, he had several rational reasons for refusing to sue for peace.

More surprisingly, there is evidence that he had a strategy in mind should his bid fail. Twice he extended an invitation to Lloyd George, known to favour the idea of exploring the possibility of peace terms, to join the War Cabinet: first on 28 May and again on 18 June 1940. Both of these dates coincide with Halifax's attempts to persuade the War Cabinet to make an approach to Hitler (through Mussolini in May, and then via the neutral Swedish government in June). Richard Lamb argues that these invitations were extended to Lloyd George because Churchill 'wanted an orderly transfer of power to an acceptable successor who would negotiate the peace'.[22] So, while arguing powerfully against such an eventuality, it seems Churchill was realistic enough to make plans should he have failed, entrusting Britain's fate in the hands of his old colleague and friend in preference to those of Halifax or Chamberlain. On both occasions Lloyd George refused to join Churchill's Cabinet, and ultimately the War Cabinet chose to support Churchill's determination not to sue for peace terms.

That he was able to bring seasoned sceptics like Halifax and Chamberlain around to accepting his arguments says something for the strength of his beliefs. His refusal even to contemplate approaching Hitler while Britain's position was so apparently hopeless may seem reckless and arrogant today. The emotion, as well as the more rational reasons, of his appeal played a crucial role, but one that is difficult to measure. Lukacs has written, 'Churchill understood something that not many people understand even now, that the greatest threat to Western Civilization was . . . Hitler.'[23] To have negotiated peace terms with the leader of such repellent ideology and morals would have compromised Britain's status and sense of herself as a democratic and liberal state. Churchill's appeal to stand firm drew on this sense of Britishness, and may go a long way to explaining how and why so many British people supported his stance against such seemingly impossible odds. Historians usually avoid writing about emotions. But Churchill's appeal – and its success – rested on emotions: fear and revulsion of Nazism, pride in Britain's past and hope that she could again defeat an aggressor state in Europe.

Questions

1. Was Churchill right to refuse to negotiate a peace settlement with Germany in the early summer of 1940?
2. Was Churchill's determination to fight on against Nazi Germany heroism or folly?

SOURCES

1. HOW DID CHURCHILL BECOME PRIME MINISTER IN MAY 1940?

Source A: letter from Bob Boothby to Churchill, 9 May 1940

Private & Confidential

Dear Winston

I have been in the House all day.
    This is the situation as I see it.

(1) The Labour party won't touch Chamberlain, at any price.

(2) Nor will Archie [Sinclair, the Liberal leader].

(3) Nor will our group.

Therefore it is inconceivable that Chamberlain can carry through a reconstruction of the Government.

   A majority of the House is, nevertheless, determined on a <u>radical</u> reconstruction, which will involve . . . the elimination of Simon and Hoare.

(4) Opinion is hardening against Halifax as Prime Minister. I am doing my best to foster this, because I cannot feel he is, in any circumstances, the right man. At the moment of writing, our group would oppose his appointment, unless it commanded universal assent.

. . . In fact, I find a gathering consensus of opinion in all quarters that you are the necessary and inevitable Prime Minister – as I wrote to you some while ago.

   God knows it is a terrible prospect for you.

   But I don't see how you can avoid it.

Yours ever

Bob

Source B: the historian Addison writing about the meeting between Chamberlain, Halifax, Margesson and Churchill on 9 May 1940

Chamberlain began by saying that he would have to resign and he was prepared to serve under either Churchill or Halifax. He implied that Churchill might not be able to win Labour support. Margesson then spoke, and may have dropped a hint that Conservative MPs would prefer Halifax. It was now for Churchill or Halifax to speak. A brief silence ensued: an invitation, perhaps, for Churchill to say that Halifax would be the candidate most likely to win the confidence of the Labour party, and that he would be proud to serve under him. But Churchill said nothing. He had received a secret pledge of support from a major Tory politician who was closely associated with Chamberlain, Kingsley Wood . . . The silence was broken by Halifax, who said that as a member of the House of Lords he could not hope to conduct a Government when the real source of authority lay in the Commons . . . [Thus] Churchill was to be Prime Minister – if, as predicted, Labour refused to serve under Chamberlain.

Source C: Churchill, writing in 1948, about the same meeting of 9 May

I have had many important interviews in my public life, and this was certainly the most important. Usually I talk a great deal, but on this occasion I was silent.

Mr Chamberlain evidently had in his mind the stormy scene in the House of Commons two nights before, when I had seemed to be in such a heated controversy with the Labour Party. Although this had been in his support and defence, he nevertheless felt that it might be an obstacle to my obtaining their adherence at this juncture. I do not recall the actual words he used, but this was the implication. His biographer, Mr Feiling, states definitely that he preferred Lord Halifax. As I remained silent a very long pause ensued . . . Then at length Halifax spoke. He said that he felt his position as a Peer . . . would make it very difficult for him to discharge the duties of Prime Minister in a war like this.

Source D: the historian Graham Stewart writing on Halifax's position

The Premiership was Halifax's for the taking. The problem was that [he] seemed reluctant to take it . . . The Premiership had not been occupied by a peer for thirty-eight years and it was understandable that as a member of the House of Lords Halifax would be apprehensive about how well he would be able to control the mood of the Commons . . . However, given both the sense of emergency and the apparent will of most MPs that he was the man best suited to tackle it, there was no bar to their changing procedures of the house so that he could speak and answer questions in the Commons . . . Such plans existed, but even if they had been more forcibly put to Halifax at the time it is doubtful whether they would have been enough to persuade him . . . In comparison to Churchill, Halifax was by his own admission relatively unschooled in military matters and as the war intensified he could expect the dynamic Churchill to be constantly seeking the upper hand on issues of strategic policy. As Halifax made clear to Chamberlain in the afternoon of 9 May, he did not wish to suffer Asquith's fate during the Great War in 1916, pushed out by his colleague Lloyd George with his more active strategies for prosecuting the war.

Source E: reaction in Whitehall to Churchill's succession to the Premiership, written by John Colville in his diary

In May 1940 the mere thought of Churchill as Prime Minister sent a cold chill down the spines of the staff at 10 Downing Street, where I was working as Assistant Private Secretary to Mr Neville Chamberlain. Churchill's impetuosity had, we thought, contributed to the Norwegian fiasco, and General Ismay had told us in despairing tones of the confusion caused by his enthusiastic irruptions into the peaceful and orderly deliberations of the Military Co-ordination Committee and the Chiefs of Staff. His verbosity and restlessness made unnecessary work, prevented real planning and caused friction.

Questions

1. Study Source B. What was the importance of Kingsley Wood's support for Churchill? (3)
2. Comment on the usefulness to a historian of Source A as evidence of the mood in the House of Commons on 9 May 1940. (5)
3. To what extent, and why, do Sources D and E disagree over the suitability of Churchill as a wartime Prime Minister? (5)
4. From Sources B and C and your own knowledge, explain the role played by both Halifax and the Labour Party in Churchill's succession to the Premiership. (5)
5. Using Sources A to E and your own knowledge, discuss the view that 'Churchill became Prime Minister by default'. (12)

Worked answer

3. Source E clearly states that Churchill's 'impetuosity' in the Military Coordination Committee had led to difficulties with the Chiefs of Staff, and even to the failure of the attempt to control Norwegian waters ('the Norwegian fiasco') in April and May 1940. The writer implies that Churchill lacked competence in the military planning necessary to conduct the war, and that he had created additional problems by being interfering and causing friction with planning staff. Source D disagrees with this interpretation, arguing that one of the main reasons for his rival Halifax bowing out of contention was his realisation that he did not have as much experience as Churchill in military matters. This, he reasoned, meant he would quickly be overshadowed and 'pushed out'. Thus it appears that Halifax believed Churchill's military talents tipped the balance in his favour as the best candidate for a wartime Prime Minister.

Source E was written by a man who had worked closely with Chamberlain as his assistant private secretary, and so it is reasonable to assume that he would have been loyal to him. His criticism of Churchill as verbose, restless and impetuous is in the same vein as Chamberlain's own criticisms of his colleague, since they were opposites in character and political style. It seems likely, therefore, that Colville was bound to be critical of Churchill's abilities. The author of Source D was trying to explain why Halifax chose to refuse the Premiership, and is thus describing Halifax's own perception of Churchill's strengths in strategic policy.

2. THE DECISION TO FIGHT ON IN 1940: RIGHT OR WRONG?

Source F: extract from the memoirs (published in 1960) of General Sir Hastings Ismay, who worked closely with Churchill throughout the war

Just before Dunkirk, the Prime Minister had asked the Chiefs of Staff for a formal expression of their views as to our ability to continue the war with any hope of success, if France were to collapse. There was no doubt in any of our minds as to what the answer would be ... The first twelve paragraphs were devoted to showing that the enemy had the whip hand in almost every sphere, and the summing-up set out in the thirteenth and final paragraph seemed somewhat inconsistent. 'Our conclusion is that, prima facie [at first sight], Germany has most of the cards; but the real test is whether the morale of our fighting personnel and civil population will counterbalance the numerical and material advantages which Germany enjoys. We believe it will.'

Source G: extract from Churchill: The End of Glory, by John Charmley

Churchill's vision of what might happen in the event of Britain failing to win can be seen from the terms of reference that he gave his Chiefs of Staff on 26 May, when he asked them to say what situation would arise in the event of 'terms being offered to Britain which would place her entirely at the mercy of Germany ... ' but what grounds were there for supposing that Germany's terms would necessarily be so Carthaginian? Were there not grounds for supposing that Hitler might be disposed to pay handsomely to avoid the perilous task of a sea and airborne invasion?

Source H: the Labour MP Hugh Dalton writing about the meeting of the Cabinet on 28 May 1940

And then he said: 'I have thought carefully in these last days whether it was part of my duty to consider entering into negotiations with That Man.' But it was idle to think that, if we tried to make peace now, we should get better terms than if we fought it out. The Germans would demand our fleet – that would be called 'disarmament' – our naval bases, and much else. We should become a slave state, though a British Government which would be Hitler's puppet would be set up – 'under Mosley or some such person' ... 'And I am convinced', he concluded, 'that every man of you would rise up and tear me down from my place if I were for one moment to contemplate parley or surrender. If this long island story of ours is to end at last, let it end only when each one of us lies choking in his own blood upon the ground.' There were loud cries of approval all round the table, in which, I think,

Amery, George Lloyd and I were loudest. Not much more was said. No one expressed even the faintest flicker of dissent.

Source I: telegram from Churchill to the French Premier, Reynaud, dated 28 May 1940

I and my colleagues . . . are convinced that at this moment when Hitler is flushed with victory and certainly counts on early and complete collapse of Allied resistance it would be impossible for Signor Mussolini to put forward proposals for a conference with any success . . . Therefore, without excluding the possibility of an approach to Signor Mussolini at some time, we cannot feel that this would be the right moment, and I am bound to add that in my opinion the effect on the morale of our people, which is now firm and resolute, would be extremely dangerous.

Source J: extract from *Five Days in London May 1940* by John Lukacs, published in 1999

Had Hitler won the Second World War we would be living in a different world. That is not arguable. What is arguable is the crucial importance of 24–28 May 1940, those five days in London . . . My argument is that Hitler was never closer to his ultimate victory than during those five days . . . *His* aim was to dominate Europe and most of European Russia – and to make or force Britain and Russia and the United States to accept such a German victory . . . In sum, Hitler could have forced his enemies to something like a draw. [But] the man in Hitler's way was Churchill. In May 1940 neither the US nor Soviet Russia was at war with Germany. At that time there *were* reasons for a British government to at least ascertain whether a temporary compromise with Hitler was at all possible. Churchill thought and said no, that even the first cautious moves would mean stepping on a slippery slope; he was right, and not only morally speaking. Had Britain stopped fighting in May 1940, Hitler would have won *his* war.

Questions

1. Study Source H. Explain who 'Mosley' was, and the significance of Churchill's reference to him in this speech. (3)
2. How far do Sources H and I agree in the tone used, and in the reasons given for the decision to fight on in May 1940? (5)
3. Study Sources F and G. What interpretation does Charmley offer of the value of the Chiefs of Staff report referred to in Source F? Why is it significant in this debate? (5)
4. To what extent do these Sources reveal the arguments and tactics used by Churchill to persuade his colleagues to fight on in May 1940? (5)

5. Using these Sources and your own knowledge, discuss the view that Churchill should have approached Mussolini to discover what peace terms Hitler may have offered Britain in May 1940. (12)

Worked answer

1. Sir Oswald Mosley was the leader of the British Union of Fascists. Churchill's reference to him in his speech to the War Cabinet was made to warn them that, should Britain submit to Germany, there were established political figures – Mosley in particular – who would gladly have taken on the leadership of a Nazi-sponsored government. Mosley's reputation was low. No doubt Churchill referred to him to illustrate how low Britain would have to stoop if she were to open negotiations with Germany, and, therefore, to stiffen the resolve of his listeners to reject such possibilities.

6

WARLORD, 1940–1945

BACKGROUND NARRATIVE

Once confirmed as Prime Minister Churchill set about creating a true National Government, including Labour, Liberal and even trade union leaders in his Cabinet. This, and his decision to appoint himself as Minister of Defence with undefined powers, dominated the character of politics for the next five years. He had more power than any Prime Minister in British history, yet he was still answerable to the Cabinet and to Parliament. The latter could remove him from office with one vote of no confidence, and Churchill was mindful of this, writing his speeches for the consumption of MPs rather than newspapers.

He centralised and streamlined government. He reduced the War Cabinet to a core of between six and nine men, none of whom had ministerial responsibilities, which left them free to consider the wide-ranging issues that the Cabinet had to decide on from day to day. By the end of 1940 the number of Cabinet committees for the civilian home front had been reduced, and the Lord President's Committee had emerged as the main body coordinating economic and social wartime policy. Chaired first by Sir John Anderson and then by Herbert Morrison (both of whom gave their name to types of civilian air-raid shelter), Churchill tended to leave domestic affairs to this committee. His inattention to major aspects of social policy has been criticised by historians and may offer one explanation for his rejection by the electorate in 1945. However, the division between military and civilian policy was not as deep as might be imagined. Both civilian and military staffs of the Cabinet Office worked and sometimes, during heavy air raids, slept in the same building. This, and the fact that the number of staff directly involved at the highest level was kept fairly small, meant issues could often be resolved quickly.

In leading the military aspects of the war, Churchill relied heavily on the Secretariat of the War Cabinet led by General Sir Hastings Ismay. He acted as liaison between Churchill and his Chiefs of Staff, with whom Churchill met almost daily. Criticism of this aspect of Churchill's leadership focuses on the way that he dominated the development of wartime strategy, perhaps to the detriment of Britain's war against Germany. Unlike Hitler or Stalin, however, Churchill did not overrule any of his Chiefs of Staff. He bullied them, and his generals, but he only got his way if he managed to persuade them that his idea was right. The way that he formulated policy was through argument and confrontation. Of one colleague he complained, 'When I thump the table and push my face towards him, what does he do? Thumps the table harder and glares back at me',[1] but he not only promoted this man to Chief of the Imperial General Staff but worked with him until the end of the war. His domination of Britain's war effort began to weaken as the war progressed. With the entry of the USSR and then the USA into the war as allies of Britain, Churchill found he had less freedom to control strategy. By 1944 he had also begun to run out of the energy for which he was famed, and verged on exhaustion until the end of the war.

ANALYSIS (1): HOW SUCCESSFULLY DID WINSTON CHURCHILL SEEK TO RALLY PUBLIC OPINION BETWEEN MAY 1940 AND MAY 1945?

During the Second World War public opinion in the combatant countries counted for more than it had ever done, since almost all the people were on the front line – fighting, working or just trying to survive. One of the other unprecedented aspects of the war was the way that the leaders of Britain, Germany, Italy and the USSR dominated its course. Each of these warlords had to rally their people to sustain the tremendous effort that was essential to support this 'total war'. Of all the warlords, Churchill had come to power last, and depended on public opinion more than any other war leader as he was the only one who could have been removed from power by a simple vote of no confidence in Parliament. But he had years of relevant experience – as a politician, writer and journalist – to draw on when he took power in May 1940. He had another great advantage: he had spent a number of years issuing warnings about the threat of Nazism to European peace. In terms of his credibility and popularity, this personal history played a crucial role.

And Churchill was astoundingly popular. Chosen not by public or even parliamentary election, his approval rating in Britain never fell below 78 per cent throughout the years he was Prime Minister, despite the disasters and setbacks of 1940–1942. Maintaining such a high level of popularity must mean that Churchill rallied opinion very successfully. Yet in the general election of July 1945 the voters rejected the Conservative Party and he lost office as the Labour Party won a landslide victory to govern peacetime Britain. Clearly Churchill's popularity was limited in some way. This analysis will attempt to explain both his successes and failures in galvanising public support.

His oratory (skill at public speaking) is most often cited as an important explanation of his popularity. With his years of experience as a journalist and politician it was a skill that he had practised and improved over forty years. He wrote his speeches himself and spent many hours finding just the right word or phrase, and rehearsing his delivery like an actor learning a part. He was, then, a skilled craftsman at speech-making by 1940. A contemporary wrote of him that 'great oratory is most often the expression of the deepest feelings of the ordinary man or woman'.[2] Taken together with a comment made by an American journalist that Churchill 'mobilised the English language and sent it into battle',[3] this helps explain the secret of Churchill's speeches.

His love of British history led him to imagine that all Britons had the same qualities of bravery and doggedness that heroes of the past had had. He did not have opinion polls to inform him of public moods but trusted (as in so many things) his instinct. The historian Jablonsky has explained this phenomenon: 'for a time in the 1940s, by dramatizing their lives and making them seem to themselves and to each other, as acting appropriately for a great historic moment, Churchill transformed the British people into a collective, romantic and heroic whole'.[4] His success was in creating an image of the historic moment, and of themselves, that people responded to. For example, in his first broadcast as Prime Minister he concluded, 'This is one of the most awe-striking periods in the long history of . . . Britain' and told his listeners that 'when the ordeal [the invasion] comes upon them, . . . [the British] will feel comfort, and even a pride, that they are sharing the perils of our lads at the Front'.[5] It's a theme that he returned to repeatedly in his speeches. 'There seems to be every reason to believe that this new kind of war is well suited to the genius and resources of the British nation', he said in a later speech, going on to list the reasons he believed the British would be hard to beat.[6]

Reading these today it seems incredibly optimistic to make such assertions when Britain and her empire alone were fighting Germany and Italy. Yet Churchill's success in stirring emotion and motivating the British people lies in those words. They both contained some element of truth in them – many British *were* brave; half million of them volunteered to join the Home Guard within a day of its formation, for example – and they held up an image of their bravery that they aspired to. The most effective propaganda contains both some truth and some popular aspiration.

His speeches were successful in other ways. Churchill was good at telling a story and in presenting complex facts in a straightforward way. Most of his speeches were narratives, telling of the progress of the war, and people got used to listening to them, or reading them, to get a sense of what was happening. He managed this without seeming condescending, and without resorting to exhortation or hypocrisy – in stark contrast to the styles used by Hitler, Mussolini and Stalin. British people found the exaggerated antics of the German and Italian dictators particularly alien, preferring explanations and 'straight talk' to their odd theatrics. Thus Churchill was able to admit that the withdrawal from Dunkirk had cost Britain dearly, sombrely declaring, 'our losses in *matériel* are enormous. We have perhaps lost one-third of the men we lost in the opening days of the battle of 21 March 1918, but we have lost nearly as many guns . . . and all our transport.'[7] This was speech-making at its most direct. No one could have been left with the impression that Dunkirk had been anything but a terrible setback to British forces and morale. Yet Churchill's standing improved throughout 1940, about which he 'said he could not quite see why he appeared so popular. After all since he came to power, everything had gone wrong and he had nothing but disasters to announce.'[8] However, this was the same man who had warned that the Czechoslovak Crisis of September 1938 had been a foretaste of a new, terrible war in Europe: 'the belief that security can be obtained by throwing a small state to the wolves is a fatal delusion. The war potential of Germany will increase more rapidly than it will be possible for France and Great Britain to complete the measures necessary for their defence.'[9] The fact that the Nazis were so spectacularly successful and that Britain was so vulnerable, by mid-1940, made Churchill appear a truthful prophet, and his reputation increased in consequence.

The care that he took to find the right words and phrases also paid dividends. Many of them are still quoted (or misquoted) today, and were popularised as slogans at the time. His pledge that 'I have nothing to offer but blood, toil, tears and sweat'[10] is well known, as is his declaration that 'We shall fight on the beaches, we shall fight on the landing grounds, we shall fight on the fields and in the streets, we shall fight in the hills; we shall never surrender.'[11] There are too many phrases and slogans to repeat here. A number of them were used on propaganda posters by the Ministry of Information for distribution across Britain and her empire. His ability to coin a phrase made his speeches all the more memorable. Determining their impact is difficult, since the BBC did not routinely monitor responses to its broadcasts. The only time it did so was for his broadcast on 15 February 1942 following the fall of Singapore, his lowest point. The approval rating of this speech was 64 per cent – a figure that seems high today, but was considered dangerously low then.[12] In all, he gave forty-nine radio broadcasts while Prime Minister, enabling him to reach a huge audience.

Film was the alternative medium to radio, and Churchill's image was developed through his appearances on newsreels in cinemas throughout the country. Unlike the carefully edited filming of Hitler, Churchill's appearances were often of him making unrehearsed visits to factories, docks or bombed cities. 'He appeared, undaunted, with a bulldog air, in a variety of costumes and hats, stomping around with a cigar and walking stick, raising the morale of cinema audiences. No such heart-warming populist appearances were made by Hitler, Stalin, not even Roosevelt.'[13] With weekly cinema attendances of 25 to 30 million during the war, this image was reaching a huge audience. Churchill 'was a showman who borrowed from the music-hall artists of his youth. Like them, he dressed up in a variety of costumes, and rejoiced in theatrical gestures like the big cigar and the V-sign.'[14] Perhaps conscious of the need to compete with the highly stylised images created by Hitler, Stalin and Mussolini, Churchill was a match for them.

He almost always wore a hat, so he would be recognisable from a distance and at times stuck it on the end of his walking stick to wave in the air above the heads of the crowd. Other props included a cigar, his V-for-Victory sign and his 'siren suits' – strange all-in-one outfits that echoed the austerity of rationed Britain. Having an image that was consistent and instantly recognisable was a requirement in the new age of daily media appearances.

However, 'Churchill was no propaganda creation'.[15] His transformation into a media hero was not a media trick. 'Everything about him proclaimed a blazingly authentic belligerence.'[16] A Ministry of Information had been established in 1939 to create propaganda to support the war effort, yet Churchill made little direct use of it himself. 'He acted as his own Minister of Morale'[17] by embarking on frequent tours of barracks and cities. The Ministry's early attempts at propaganda were embarrassingly amateur and it became the butt of many jokes, but by 1942 it was producing very effective propaganda, basing its work on the findings of its social surveys. It had also begun to raise the issues of Britain's war aims and post-war future.

Churchill did not like this and spent a lot of energy complaining to the Minister of Information, his friend Brendan Bracken, about this policy. His objections were twofold: that raising expectations about the post-war years was irresponsible given that the winning of the war should come first; and that there was little chance Britain would be able to afford such huge reconstruction and social projects. His appeal to the public did not rest on promises and policies for the future. 'In Churchill's mind there was little connection between the morale of the general public and promises of better social conditions after the war . . . for him, morale was associated with such factors of everyday life as food, rest and transport.'[18] It's for this reason that he was opposed to the rationing of food and clothing – probably the best example of his failure to understand all the moods of the British people. Many regarded rationing not as Churchill did, as being unnecessarily drastic, but as being fair to all. For some, rationing led to a great improvement in their standard of living. Churchill had a blind spot for certain issues that the public felt were important and which he did not. So whereas his frequent visits to different parts of the country and impromptu chats with ordinary people did gain him a reputation for being aware of, and empathetic to, the strains of everyday life, he was clearly out of tune in other ways.

One criticism that is made of his leadership is that he concentrated on the military prosecution of the war almost to the exclusion of domestic matters. These he left to the Defence Committee for Supply under the leadership of Anderson, and then Morrison. This distance meant he failed to appreciate the changing attitudes of society during these formative years of war. As a result, Churchill went into the 1945 election with a manifesto that seemed weak and irrelevant in comparison with that of the Labour Party, many of whom had come to dominate domestic politics during the war. They campaigned for social welfare, economic planning and nationalisation – and won.

Churchill's achievement was to rally the British public to supporting the most comprehensive and demanding war effort that Britain has ever known, in conditions that ranged from life threatening to austere. There was, of course, still dissatisfaction and opposition from some. But his simple approach revealed his genuine commitment and emotion enough for many to identify with it themselves. His approval rating was consistently higher than that of his government. Most telling is that even in June 1945 an opinion poll revealed that 48 per cent wanted Churchill to continue as Prime Minister after the general election. Attlee, who, as leader of Labour, became Prime Minister after the election, scored only 13 per cent. This surely demonstrates the paradox of Churchill's popularity and success at rallying public support: that it was personal and deeply felt, yet empty once the emergency of war had begun to recede.

Questions

1. Why, despite his popularity as a war leader, did Churchill fail to build a credible reputation as a peacetime Prime Minister?
2. What contribution did Churchill's coalition government make to the policies for the reconstruction of post-war Britain?

ANALYSIS (2): DID CHURCHILL SACRIFICE TOO MUCH FOR THE GRAND ALLIANCE?

Richard Overy has written, 'Canonised as the saviour of Western Civilisation, vilified as the flawed commander who diminished the empire he led, Churchill defies neutrality.'[19] The extremity of these two reputations – saviour or wrecker – dominates an analysis of Churchill's relationship with the USA and the USSR. The issues are emotive: did Churchill sacrifice the British Empire, Britain's great power status, her economic strength and the independence of Eastern Europe all for his obsession with defeating Hitler? A number of revisionist historians – Charmley in particular – have raised these accusations against him. Others – including Lukacs – defend him, stating that the price paid for victory over Nazi Germany was worth paying, given that regime's unlawful and immoral character. Yet other historians point out that by 1940 Churchill's freedom of action was so severely restricted that he had no choice but to make the sacrifices necessary for alliances with the USSR and USA. The alternative was to surrender completely.

Churchill did not create the Grand Alliance. His best efforts had failed to convince Roosevelt to declare war against Germany, and Britain and her empire had fought on alone from the French surrender in June 1940 until June 1941. Unexpectedly, Britain's first ally turned out to be the USSR, and this came about because of Hitler's invasion of his former ally on 22 June 1941. That evening Churchill broadcast over the radio, offering immediate aid to the Soviets to fight against Germany. Over the next few months the Soviet–British relationship developed until they signed a Treaty of Friendship in May 1942. Churchill was no friend of communism or the Soviet Union, yet he chose to sacrifice his strong ideological objections to ally with one cruel dictator – Stalin – to defeat another – Hitler. He considered Hitler to be the worse evil and once explained that 'if Hitler invaded Hell, I would at least make a favourable reference to the Devil in the House of Commons'. It was an apt comment for him to make, having been so opposed to Bolshevism that he had wanted to 'strangle it at birth' in 1918. Being allied to 'the Devil' had a high cost. By 1945 relations with Stalin had deteriorated, and the division of Europe into Soviet and Western spheres of influence was well under way, and dominated the second half of the twentieth century.

Relations with the Soviets were never going to be easy. They had been cut off from mainstream international relations for several years before 1939 and were predisposed to distrusting any Western government. And the relationship was put under almost immediate strain by Churchill's and then Roosevelt's refusal to open a second front in Europe. Along the Eastern Front Soviet troops were bearing the brunt of the German forces' attacks, but Churchill refused to commit British troops there, preferring to concentrate instead on campaigning in the Mediterranean and North Africa. Once Roosevelt had declared war, he supported Churchill's stance – at least until 1943, by which time the damage to the relationship with Stalin had been done. Convinced that the decision was a deliberate ploy to bleed the USSR dry of men and supplies by leaving them to fight Germany alone in Europe, Stalin grew to distrust every promise or statement made by his supposed allies.

Churchill resisted the idea of committing British troops to the east because he knew that Britain did not have enough resources – men or *matériel* – to be able to fight on more than one front. And he identified the Mediterranean and North African arena as being of greater importance to British and imperial interests. It was there that access to India, and imperial control, was threatened. So, although he acknowledged that the USSR was having to resist Germany's fighting forces alone, he refused to sacrifice his strategic priorities in order to help them out. Thus, when Stalin first requested (on 19 July 1941) that a second European front be opened, Churchill refused, and went on refusing until 1944.

In sticking to his strategic priorities at the expense of his Soviet ally Churchill found, however, that he had to make some unpleasant concessions. By 1942 he realised that 'diplomatic appeasement of the Russians was the only thing which he had left to offer',[20] and shrank from opposing Stalin's territorial demands in Eastern Europe. In fact, by early 1942 Churchill was suggesting that Britain and the USA meet those demands, to keep the USSR in the war, but knowing that 'the Soviets had thereby gained a possible free hand in determining the future of much of Europe'.[21] This capitulation to Stalin's territorial greed is partly explained by the fact that 1942 was a year of military setbacks for a weakening Britain, and that neither she nor the USA was going to be able to launch a new campaign in Europe until 1943 at the earliest. It was not, in other words, a question of Churchill making sacrifices to the USSR unnecessarily. It was certainly a risk, and one that he lost. In the end, the future of Eastern Europe – including Poland, for which Britain had declared war in the first place – was handed over to the Soviets.

'Nevertheless, if the longest view is taken, Churchill's strategic dealings with Stalin may be judged to have served Britain's interests very well indeed.'[22] Where it suited his perceptions of Britain's strategic needs, Churchill was able to secure two important points. The first was the joint partition with the USSR of Persia (Iran) in August 1941. Despite Persian neutrality Churchill agreed to invade and partition it to secure its oil supplies for the Allies, and to prevent them from falling into German hands. It also reinforced Britain's valuable hold over the Middle East, where control of the Suez Canal was vital to securing supplies to and from India and the Far East. The second was the so-called 'Naughty Document' of October 1944. During a visit to Moscow Churchill proposed a demarcation of British and Soviet spheres of influence, suggesting a fifty–fifty share of Yugoslavia and almost total British influence over Greece. Stalin agreed to this; it probably appealed to his unscrupulous character. He also stuck to it, allowing Britain to intervene in the Greek civil war in 1944 to defeat communist forces, and letting her actively support Tito in Yugoslavia. Although nominally communist, Tito turned out to be an independent influence in a region that came to be dominated by Soviet-controlled puppet governments. This and the restoration of Greece to an authoritarian, but non-communist, government meant that the Balkans were never totally controlled by the USSR, even at the height of the Cold War, and British dominance in the Mediterranean continued. About this agreement Carlton has written, 'the truth seems to be that at a time of great national weakness Churchill, without a single card in his hand, effectively bluffed Stalin into giving him a free hand in Greece'.[23]

Sparring with Stalin was no mean feat, but Churchill had enough guile to meet the challenge. With Roosevelt he faced a different challenge. His eventual disappointment in Roosevelt's response to the war was almost equal to his conviction that without the USA's involvement, Germany could not be defeated. It has been argued that he was so desperate for the Americans to enter the war that he was prepared to sacrifice too much to them. Yet when the USA was forced into the war in December 1941, Roosevelt agreed to fight against (and defeat) Germany first in Europe, which was a considerable sacrifice on his part, as the most direct threat to his country was from the Japanese in the Pacific. But he drove a hard bargain with Britain. Even before entering the war he had insisted on Britain handing over some of her naval bases and financial assets in return for a supply of fifty old destroyers – ships that were found to be out of date and almost useless. The toughness of his bargains stemmed from suspicions that many of Churchill's tactics – his strategic concentration on the Mediterranean, for example – came from his desire to expand British imperial possessions. Churchill, in his turn, came to believe that the quarrels over empire masked America's own imperial aspirations.

Charmley has argued that American pressure pushed Churchill to begin to dismantle the British Empire during the war, against all his principles as an imperialist. He states that Cripps's mission to India in 1942 was a direct response to pressure from Roosevelt to give independence to Britain's most important colony. The visit led to political unrest and the 'Quit India' campaign. But Indian nationalism was not created by his visit. With or without the war, India had been increasingly difficult for Britain to govern, and Britain's will to govern her empire had been weakening in the changing political climate of the inter-war years. Constitutional reforms were being made to colonies throughout the war and were part of 'a process that had its roots deep in colonial history and which was consistent with the . . . measured devolutionary progress' already being carried out by the pre-war Colonial Office.[24] The post-war changes that transformed the British Empire were already under way before the war had begun. But the war undoubtedly accelerated this process and more so than American pressures on British policy there.

Churchill did, of course, understand that in accepting the ideology of Roosevelt's foreign policy he ran the risk of stirring up nationalist feeling in the British Empire. He had attempted to exclude the empire from the implications of the Atlantic Charter's declaration on the peoples of liberated Europe. He knew that promising them the right to choose their own governments and at the same time denying that right to people who lived in British colonies was politically impossible. But equally he had to maintain good relations with the USA to fight the war, and so he sacrificed his own deeply held imperialism to this. As significant was his agreement to Roosevelt's policy of insisting on the 'unconditional surrender' of

Germany before any negotiation of peace could take place. This was a concession to American pressure that had much longer-term consequences than perhaps Churchill imagined. In his eagerness to please Roosevelt, he committed Britain to a principle that 'ensured that the fighting would stop with Soviet troops on German soil'.[25] It meant that Stalin's troops would be occupying most of Eastern Europe by war's end, and would be in an excellent position to push the borders of the USSR deep into the heart of Europe, placing her in a much more powerful position than in 1939.

By war's end Britain found herself in no position to be able to counter the challenge of a more powerful USSR. Fighting the war had bankrupted Britain by March 1941, and she was able to pay for that month's supplies only after a loan from the Belgian government in exile in London. Henceforth she was dependent on American economic support to survive. Charmley argues that this position stripped Britain of her pre-war wealth, leaving her unable to afford to maintain her empire afterwards. Yet it was Roosevelt who persuaded the American Congress to make an unprecedented offer – to send supplies to Britain but accept payment after the war had finished. This Lend–Lease scheme also came at a price: its abrupt end once the war was over and the need to pay it all back. Agreeing to it, 'Churchill had no doubt that he had mortgaged Britain's future'.[26] But without it Britain would have had to withdraw from the war. In the event Britain found that she had to pay back only $650 million of the $27,023 million she had received during the war. However, this was negotiated only after the USA had abruptly stopped the Lend–Lease, and when it was obvious that Britain was simply unable to afford any more.[27]

For Charmley, Churchill's determination to continue to fight Hitler's Germany was the cause of this desperate situation: 'the Prime Minister's policy of 1940 had, in effect, failed. Far from securing Britain's independence, it had mortgaged it to America'.[28] But the alternative would have been not to fight and to attempt survival in a Nazi Europe, with no guarantee of security for Britain or her empire. Lukacs has countered Charmley's argument with the statement that 'Churchill saw the choice clearly; either all of Europe dominated by Germany, or – at worst – the eastern half of Europe dominated by Russia; and half of Europe was better than none.'[29] Churchill consistently believed Nazi Germany to be the worse evil, and the greater threat to Britain, and this dominated his wartime policy and military strategy. But he was not alone in these choices: 'The coalition survived through a common interest in the defeat of Germany and little else.'[30] All three partners had to make unpalatable sacrifices to ensure the defeat of Hitler's Germany. For Britain this period coincided with, and perhaps accelerated, her decline as a great power. But her participation in the war and the sacrifices Churchill made during its course were not the causes of this decline.

Questions

1. 'Churchill in his time was overestimated as a military leader and underestimated in civilian affairs.' Discuss this view in relation to his years as Prime Minister, 1940–1945.
2. What was Churchill's legacy to post-war Britain?

SOURCES

1. CHURCHILL'S WARTIME IMAGE

Source A: Churchill on the steps of No. 10, May 1940

[see following page]

Source B: General Sir Hastings Ismay worked very closely with Churchill during the war; this is an extract from his memoirs, published in 1960

The RAF Operations Room of No. 11 Group, Fighter Command, was Churchill's favourite port of call at this period. It was the nerve centre from which he could follow the course of the whole air battle. The sequent to a visit in mid-August must be told. There had been heavy fighting throughout the afternoon; at one moment every single squadron in the Group was engaged; there was nothing in reserve, and the map table showed new waves of attackers crossing the coast. I felt sick with fear. As the evening closed in the fighting died down, and we left by car for Chequers. Churchill's first words were: 'Don't speak to me; I have never been so moved.' After about five minutes he leaned forward and said, 'Never in the field of human conflict has so much been owed by so many to so few.' The words burned into my brain and I repeated them to my wife when I got home. Churchill, too, had evidently photographed them in his mind; for, as everyone knows, he used them in a speech that was heard throughout the world.

Source C: extract from a speech made by Churchill on 18 June 1940, showing its layout

[see p. 99]

Figure 6 Churchill on the steps of No. 10

```
Upon this battle depends the
    survival of Christian civilization.

Upon it depends our own British life
    and the long continuity of our
    institutions, and our Empire.

The whole fury and might of the enemy
    must very soon be turned on us.

Hitler knows that he will hv to break
    us in this Island, or lose the war.

If we can stand up to him,
    all Europe may be freed,
        and the life of the world
            may move forward into
                broad and sunlit uplands.

But if we fail,
    then the whole world,
        including the United States,
            and all that we have known and
                                cared for,
            will sink into the abyss of a
                new Dark Age
                made more sinister and
                perhaps more prolonged by
                    the lights of perverted
                                Science.

Let us therefore brace ourselves to
    our duty, and so bear ourselves that
        if the British Empire and
            Commonwealth lasts for a
                thousand years, men will still
                say,

    'This was their finest hour'.
```

Figure 7 'This was their finest hour' speech. With permission of Churchill College, Cambridge

Source D: extract from 'Churchill and the Cinema' by D. J. Wenden

Film appearances could be more frequent and could catch him on the hoof with none of the agonizing preparation needed for a speech. The nation saw him doing his job, conferring with Allied leaders, visiting warriors at home and abroad, touring docks, dwellings and factories. He could speak personally with only a limited number of men and women on the street. Newsreel and documentary footage enabled almost all to feel his personality, to believe that they knew him and he knew them. Churchill's premiership was a shared experience in a way that Lloyd George's equally vital role in 1917–18 had never been.

Source E: official war photograph

The official caption for this reads: 'THE PRIME MINISTER'S TOUR. Mr Churchill has just concluded a tour in which he saw bomb damage, inspected ARP [air-raid precautions] workers, visited factories and docks. He was accompanied by Mrs Churchill and received a tremendous welcome wherever he went.

Photo shows: while touring a docks area the PM saw two workmen having their dinner. Alluding to their well-filled plates, he asked: "Are you managing to get plenty of food?" "Aye, Sir, we're doing grand, thank you," was the reply.'

Figure 8 Churchill and two dockers

Source F: official war photograph

The official caption for this reads: 'A FRENCHMAN LIGHTS A FAMOUS CIGAR. As a gesture of welcome, a Frenchman leans forward to light Prime Minister Winston Churchill's cigar during the British leader's tour of Cherbourg to see the reconstruction work now going on.'

Source G: official wartime poster, 'Let us go forward together'

[see following page]

Questions

1. Read Source C. What can the historian learn about Churchill's oratory from this source? (5)
2. What further information can Source B add to an under-standing of Churchill's skills as a speech-maker? (3)
3. What impressions do Sources B and E give of Churchill's wartime leadership? (5)
4. Using Sources A and G, explain the characteristics of Churchill's public image. (5)
5. Using any two or more of these Sources, explain the different ways in which Churchill's image was created and sustained. (12)

"LET US GO FORWARD TOGETHER"

Worked answer

1. What this Source reveals most clearly is information about Churchill's oratorical style. The way that the speech, one of his more famous and quoted, has been typed out as if it were a poem shows that Churchill paid as much attention to how he was going to deliver it as to its content. This document displays the results of Churchill's dedication to practising the delivery of this speech, with each line laid out in the way that it was to be spoken, with pauses indicated by punctuation and new lines. Churchill was renowned for his skill and attention in choosing words and phrases that sounded 'right'. Thus in one of the most famous passages of this speech his words carry not only the right meaning, but also the right sound. When describing 'good' elements, he uses words with open sounds, such as 'broad', 'sunlit' and 'uplands'. When describing Nazi Germany, he used words that sound closed and can be hissed with great vehemence, such as 'abyss' and 'sinister'. For the historian this document reveals the attention to detail that Churchill paid to his speech-making, and the fact that he would read from a prepared script, rather than ad-lib.

2. CHURCHILL, THE USA AND THE USSR

Source H: Churchill's speech, broadcast on 22 June 1941, on the day of the German invasion of the USSR

At four o'clock this morning Hitler attacked and invaded Russia . . . Hitler is a monster of wickedness, insatiable in his lust for blood and plunder. Not content with having all Europe under his heel, or else terrorized into various forms of abject submission, he must now carry his work of butchery and desolation among the vast multitudes of Russia and of Asia . . . The Nazi regime is indistinguishable from the worst features of Communism . . . No-one has been a more consistent opponent of Communism than I have for the last twenty-five years. I will unsay no word that I have spoken about it. But all this fades away before the spectacle which is now unfolding . . . Any man or state who fights on against Nazidom will have our aid . . . It follows, therefore, that we shall give whatever help we can to Russia and the Russian people.

Source I: Churchill's speech of 24 August 1941, broadcast following his first meeting with Roosevelt at Placentia Bay

The meeting was therefore symbolic . . . It symbolises . . . the deep underlying unities which stir and at decisive moments rule the English-speaking peoples throughout the world. Would it be presumptuous for me to say that it symbolises something even more majestic – namely: the marshalling of the good forces of the world against the evil forces which are now so formidable and triumphant and which have cast their cruel spell over the whole of Europe and a large part of Asia?

This was a meeting which marks for ever in the pages of history the taking-up by the English-speaking nations, amid all this peril, tumult and confusion, of the guidance of the fortunes of the broad toiling masses in all the continents; and our loyal effort without any clog of selfish interest to lead them forward out of the miseries into which they have been plunged back to the broad highroad of freedom and justice. This is the highest honour and the most glorious opportunity which could ever have come to any branch of the human race.

Source J: extract from the diary of John Colville, private secretary to Churchill, published in 1985

Friday, February 23rd [1945]
The PM was rather depressed, thinking of the possibilities of Russia one day turning against us, saying that Chamberlain had trusted Hitler as he was now trusting Stalin (though he thought in different circumstances) . . .

Now, however, 'the shadows of victory' were upon us. In 1940 the issue was clear and he could see distinctly what was to be done. But when Harris [Commander in Chief of RAF Bomber Command] had finished his destruction of Germany, 'What will lie between the white snows of Russia and the white cliffs of Dover?' . . . After the war, continued the PM, we should be weak, we should have no money and no strength and we should lie between the two great powers of the USA and the USSR.

Source K: John Charmley's critical assessment of Churchill's policy towards his allies, from Churchill: The End of Glory, published in 1993

The German invasion of Russia offered Churchill the only road out of the impasse he was in: with 'victory' nowhere in sight and the Americans seemingly oblivious to the future of the British Empire, Russia offered him an ally and the hope that German pressure on Egypt and the Suez Canal would be lifted. This was why Churchill hastened unheeding to the support of Stalin . . . Underneath it all was one simple fact: the Prime Minister's policy of 1940 had, in effect, failed. Far from securing Britain's independence, it had mortgaged it to America . . . In his haste to secure short-term advantages, Churchill had neglected to ask himself what political implications his generous rhetorical offers of help to the Soviets might carry. As with the Americans, he too readily assumed the Russians would put aside other considerations in the common struggle; but of all the Allied leaders, he was the only one who consistently allowed his horizons to be bound entirely by short- and medium-term considerations.

Questions

1. Read Source H. Explain Churchill's motives for offering aid to the Soviet Union in June 1941, with reference to this Source. (5)
2. Read Source I. In what ways does the tone of this speech differ from that in Source H? (5)
3. How useful is Source J as evidence of Churchill's own assessment of relations with the USSR and the USA? (5)
4. Using Sources H to K and your own knowledge, discuss the assertion that Churchill 'consistently allowed his horizons to be bound entirely by short- and medium-term considerations' when dealing with the USA and the USSR during the Second World War. (15)

Worked answer

3. Although not published until the mid-1980s, John Colville's diaries were written during the Second World War, breaking all the rules of secrecy. They are, therefore, a contemporary record written by one of the people who worked very closely with Churchill. The extract is useful in that it records Churchill's reflections made just after the Yalta Conference on Britain's current and future position. At that conference it had become obvious that Britain had lost its role as the chief member of the 'Grand Alliance' and that power had shifted to the USA and the USSR, the Allies with the bulk of the fighting forces in Europe. His comment that 'in 1940 the issue was clear' implies that by 1945 he felt the issues to be much less clear and perhaps even to be beyond his understanding.

The value of this source comes from its intimacy with Churchill, revealing how even then he thought aloud, forming phrases in case of the need to make a speech: 'the white snows of Russia and the white cliffs of Dover'. It gives a flavour of the way his thinking was developing, of his having to grapple with post-war realities once Germany had been defeated. That he compared his actions to those of Chamberlain shows that not only was this a very private conversation (he would never have admitted this in public), but that he was 'rather' depressed. Churchill was, however, prone to bouts of such depression, and so a historian has to treat this Source with some care. It is evidence of one particular exchange, and not of a wholesale change in policy.

7

CONTROVERSIES

BACKGROUND NARRATIVE

Churchill's long career is full of controversial episodes, from his involvement in the Tonypandy incident of 1910 to the decision to create a British hydrogen bomb in the 1950s. Because of this, his career offers many episodes that could be the focus of personal studies for AS and A2 History, as they are the subject of so much contemporary and historiographical interpretation.

This chapter looks at two controversies of his wartime leadership: the decision to bomb Dresden in 1945, and the decision not to bomb the death camp at Auschwitz in 1944–1945.

ANALYSIS (1): WHAT ROLE DID CHURCHILL PLAY IN THE DEBATE OVER WHETHER TO BOMB AUSCHWITZ?

'We are in the presence of a crime without a name.'[1] This was Churchill's reaction to the first reports of the routine mass killings that were taking place on the Eastern Front as the Nazis advanced on Moscow in the summer of 1941. He had learned of these killings from summaries produced for him by the British Secret Intelligence Service, based upon the work of their decoders. Churchill was convinced of the importance of intelligence gained from the decoding of German communications – he had played a key role in the development of British code-breaking since the First World War – and relied on these weekly summaries for information on Nazi strategy. The extent of what Churchill, the British and the other Allies knew, from their own intelligence sources as well as others, is at the core of this issue. The question of bombing Auschwitz could not arise until several conditions had been fulfilled: the British needed to know and understand that Auschwitz was a death camp; the camp had to be within the bombing range of Allied aircraft and bases; and the Allies had to agree that it was a priority target.

In his book on this topic, Gilbert suggests that the British did not know the true function of Auschwitz as the main death camp until June 1944. He shows that although information about the camp was known before then, it was not enough to enable the British to identify that it was a death camp for the execution of Jews and other peoples detested by Hitler's regime. This was because Auschwitz was not one camp, but a complex of three camps. The information that the British had decoded before June 1944 had come from only two of the camps: Auschwitz, the concentration camp where people were imprisoned, worked and starved to death; and Monowitz, the I.G. Farben synthetic oil factory operated by the prisoners. Information about Birkenau – the death camp – was not intercepted by the British, since it was not Nazi practice to report the number of people who were taken directly to the gas chambers to be killed, only those who had been selected for labour. This partial information was only completed by the reports of two eyewitnesses from the camp (Rudolf Vrba and Alfred Wetzler) who managed to escape in the spring of 1944.

There seems to be no published record of when Churchill first read the Vrba–Wetzler accounts about Auschwitz although extracts were broadcast by the BBC on 18 June 1944. He does not mention Auschwitz, or the accounts of these two escapees in his history of the war, but does comment on the deportation of the Hungarian Jews (taking place at that time) to it. Of their fate he wrote, 'There is no doubt that this is probably the greatest and most horrible crime ever committed in the whole history of the world, and it has been done by scientific machinery by nominally civilised men.'[2] It seems clear, then, that by June 1944 Churchill understood that Auschwitz was not just a concentration camp, but a death camp. However, the impetus to take action came not from Churchill but from outside his government.

On 6 July, following a meeting with members of the Jewish Agency, Eden reported to Churchill that he had agreed to examine the idea of bombing the railway lines that led to Auschwitz, and the camp itself. He also asked if Churchill would approach Stalin to issue a warning to the Hungarian government to stop the deportations. Churchill promptly agreed to both of these suggestions, and on the following day Eden wrote to Sinclair of the Air Ministry to request a report on the feasibility of a bombing raid. Sinclair's response was to reject the idea: 'I am advised that (a) [bombing the railway lines that led to the camp] is out of our power. It is only by an enormous concentration of bomber forces that we have been able to interrupt communications in Normandy; the distance of Silesia from our bases entirely rules out our doing anything of the kind.'[3] Bombing the camp itself was out of the range of the RAF, and so the issue was forwarded to the Americans for their consideration, since their air force was within range. At this point no one in Britain knew that the Americans had already rejected the possibility of bombing Auschwitz just a few days earlier. However, Sinclair did suggest an alternative strategy of dropping weapons over the camp in the hope that some would reach the prisoners and they would be able to rebel or escape. This was something that had worked with some success in March 1944 at Amiens Prison when 150 prisoners had managed to escape following a weapons drop from the air.

But Eden did not pursue this suggestion and it is uncertain if Churchill ever knew of it. Churchill had to rely on his ministers to bring matters like this to his attention, as it was clearly impossible for him to be aware of every event, possibility or policy. Both Gilbert and Breitman identify the Foreign Office as being the most responsible for the inaction and anti-Semitism that surrounded this debate. Some of the key Foreign Office officials betrayed prejudice of Jews. Cavendish-Bentinck's comments were typical of this attitude: 'The Poles, and to a far greater extent the Jews, tend to exaggerate German atrocities in order to stoke us up.'[4] This prejudice often combined with Foreign Office concerns over Jewish emigration to Palestine and the effects that this was having on the Arab population there. When requests for intelligence about Auschwitz were requested from the Foreign Office by the Air Ministry nothing was received for several weeks. By the time a further request had been made, the Foreign Office had concluded that the deportations from Hungary had stopped, and the sense of urgency was lost. Researching Auschwitz as a bombing target was no longer a priority and the idea was dropped.

Undoubtedly, bombing Auschwitz would have been an operation full of risk: for the air crews, but also for the prisoners in the camp, since there was no guarantee that they would benefit from air raids that were just as likely to kill them as their Nazi captors. There was also great concern about the possibility of reprisals, for which the Nazi regime had developed a taste. British intelligence was estimating that about 160,000 British and 30,000 Americans were being held prisoner by the Nazis at this time, and feared they would be subjected to the arbitrary executions favoured by their captors as reprisals for raids on the camp. It was just as possible that camp inmates could be subjected to similar reprisals. In all, the idea of bombing Auschwitz struck at the heart of the controversy of bombing strategy. The Allies needed to be able to claim that their raids were aimed at targets of military importance, not at civilian populations, or as reprisals for Nazi acts, so that they could claim the moral high ground. At the time that Churchill, Eden and Sinclair were considering the possibility, Auschwitz had not been identified as being of importance to the Nazi war effort, and thus any bombing of it would have fallen outside their self-imposed rule. Earlier discussions about launching air raids as reprisals for the deportation of Poles had raised this same dilemma. The Air Chief, Charles Portal, described it: 'We have, I think, always insisted that air attacks are ordinary operations of war against military (including of course industrial) targets, and intended to destroy the enemy's war output. We have thus deprecated the carrying out of air attacks as reprisals.'[5]

Had the Allies known more about the operations of the camp, they may have been able to make a case for its importance to the 'enemy's war output', since from July, inmates had begun to be shipped out of the camp to supplement the labour force in Germany's munitions industry. Perhaps even more frustrating was the fact that on 18 July 1944 the US Air Force (USAAF) designated the Monowitz factory as a bombing target for the first time because of its role in the production of synthetic oil. Only five miles away from Auschwitz–Birkenau, it was bombed six times, with small losses for the air crews but causing only temporary damage to the factory. Some of these raids resulted in accidental hits on Auschwitz, and caused more deaths and serious injury for camp inmates than for their SS guards. So not only was bombing an inexact weapon, it was also one full of moral dilemmas.

Of course, Churchill and his government could not have decided to bomb Auschwitz without American support, since it was their air force that was within range of the region. But the Americans had rejected the idea of bombing the camp or the railways leading to it before the British, and when it was resubmitted to them in July, they rejected it again. Stalin gave and then refused permission for the British and Americans to use the Soviet air base at Poltava to run missions to drop supplies and weapons to the Poles during the Warsaw Uprising, and restricted his involvement in the debate over Auschwitz to issuing a verbal warning to the Nazis that war crimes would be punished. In general, the Allies were much more comfortable with issuing warnings than taking action. The Allied Declaration of December 1942, and Eden's statement that 'The only truly effective means of succouring the tortured Jewish, and I may add, the other suffering peoples of Europe, lies in an Allied victory'[6] were typical of this response. The war was being fought on a truly global scale and 'the stakes of the military conflict were so high that many government officials and private citizens wanted to focus all efforts and attention on the overall task. They paid little attention to anything else, particularly if it might complicate winning the war as quickly as possible.'[7]

Churchill's focus was clearly on winning the war. He 'inevitably dealt far more with larger questions of military and diplomatic strategy and of the Allied partnership than with specific decisions about rescue of Jews'.[8] But he had made a specific request that the idea of bombing Auschwitz be investigated. From an initially cautious response from the Air Ministry, the Foreign Office had been asked for more information, and this they failed to provide. The full story of why this was so may not be revealed for some time yet, since a number of the files are still kept secret. The calculations about the effectiveness of raids over Auschwitz appear oddly clinical, given what we now know about the suffering inflicted there, and any justification for the failure to take action seems inadequate in the light of that knowledge.

Questions

1. How and why was Britain's response to the Holocaust affected by imperial considerations?
2. Why is the issue of the bombing of Auschwitz still a controversial one today?

ANALYSIS (2): WHAT ROLE DID CHURCHILL PLAY IN THE CONTROVERSIAL DECISION TO BOMB THE CITY OF DRESDEN IN FEBRUARY 1945?

The historian of Bomber Command has written: 'to those who planned and directed it, the raid on Dresden was no different from scores of other operations mounted during the years of the war . . . it was impossible to anticipate the firestorm which developed, multiplying the usual devastation and deaths a hundredfold'.[9] This raid 'aroused a revulsion even in the dying days of the war which has not been diminished by the passing of a generation'.[10] On the night of 13 and 14 February 1945 805 aircraft of the RAF attacked Dresden, in eastern Germany. On the following day 600 bombers of the USAAF carried out daylight raids, even strafing fleeing people with machine-guns. The fires burned so ferociously that the temperature rose above 1,800 degrees Fahrenheit. No exact figure for the dead can be agreed because the ferocity of the fires left little to identify, and estimates range from 25,000 to 135,000 people killed by the firestorm. People were still clearing the bodies two months later, by which time they had to resort to clearing what remained in the shelters by using flamethrowers. A beautiful and ancient city had been reduced to ruins overnight. Yet 'the strategic impact of the raid appears to have been slight. Trains were running through Dresden within two days. Vital war factories, such as the electronic plant at Dresden-Neusiedlitz, were unscathed.'[11] But hospitals had been destroyed and thousands of refugees from the east, who had been camping out in the city, had been killed, including a high number of children and women.

On watching newsreels of the effects of British air raids over German cities in 1941 Churchill had suddenly exclaimed, 'Are we beasts? Are we taking this too far?'[12] Four years later he was to face evidence of even worse devastation than anything the RAF had been capable of carrying out in 1941, yet he was clearly responsible for the policy that had led to the raids over Dresden.

Allied bombing of German cities has proved to be one of the most controversial aspects of their strategy, and the raid over Dresden has come to symbolise what was wrong with that strategy. This analysis will examine Churchill's role in the development of the policies of strategic and area bombing that led to this raid, and his particular responsibility for the decision to attack Dresden itself.

Soon after the beginning of the war, Churchill had declared that Britain's 'supreme effort must be to gain overwhelming mastery in the air. The Fighters are our salvation, but the Bombers alone provide the means to victory.'[13] He gave industrial priority to the construction of bombers at a time when British materials were at their lowest point. This seemed to confirm his reputation as someone who was a committed proponent of aerial warfare. Since the first developments in flight, he had been fascinated by its potential (as he was by most technical inventions). As First Lord of the Admiralty (1911–1915) he had developed a Naval Air Service. As Secretary of State for Air (1919–1921) he had supported the establishment of the Royal Air Force as an independent service, supported the development of long-range flying and introduced the use of air power as a method of imperial control. His experiment with an Air Force Administration of Iraq (using air raids to stifle unrest) taught him that aerial control was far cheaper than using the army and in this case, had been more effective, too. His campaigning to improve and increase Britain's defence, especially aerial defence, in the 1930s led to his appointment to the Air Defence Research Committee in 1935, despite being out of political favour.

So it is unsurprising that once war broke out in 1939 Churchill was firmly in favour of using the RAF. 'Where Chamberlain as Prime Minister refused to unleash the air weapon, Churchill had no such scruples.'[14] The Air Ministry supported him in this as they were keen to prove the importance of aerial combat as an independent weapon, and not one that simply supported the actions of the army or navy ('tactical bombing') on the front line of battle. They wanted to test their ideas for bombing deep inside enemy territory ('strategic bombing') to cause industrial and social havoc. Of course, this meant bombing civilians. 'Strategic bombing was an extremely aggressive doctrine which depended on relentless and ruthless prosecution for success.'[15] Churchill was certainly ruthless enough, and the German 'Blitz' of 1940–1941 over Britain's cities made strategic bombing more acceptable to the British public, too. With the appointment of Arthur Harris as Commander of Bomber Command, the RAF had found someone who was also ruthless – and relentless – in his belief that German cities had to be hit. This practice of targeting the general region of a city became known as 'area bombing' and is the most controversial strategy of all, since its overriding purpose was to attack people in their homes to reduce their morale.

Churchill was less relentless than Harris in the prosecution of area bombing. In September 1941 he commented that, 'It is a very disputable factor in the present war. On the contrary, all that we have learnt since the war began shows that its effects, both physical and moral, are greatly exaggerated.'[16] But the bombing continued since it was the only means for Britain to attack Germany. After the entry of the USSR into the war as an ally, bombing took on even more importance: while fighting raged along the Eastern Front and the Soviets bore the brunt of the Nazi war machine, Britain and, later, the USA offered bombing as their contribution to the war effort. 'If there had been no bomber offensive . . . would it have been possible for the Allies to justify the interminable delay before opening the Second Front in Europe?'[17]

Thoughts of the Soviets weighed heavily on this issue throughout the war. From 1942, when Churchill had flown to Moscow to break the news to Stalin that Britain and the USA would not be opening a second front in Western Europe that year, he had offered bombing as one of the compensatory campaigns. Stalin had liked the idea, even giving suggestions of cities worth targeting. And so the bombing offensive continued to take priority. With the launch of the second front on D-Day in June 1944, Allied bombing had to be diverted to provide tactical support for the troops invading France. But 'as Churchill prepared to leave for Yalta for the last major Allied conference of the European war, he turned almost impulsively to consider what evidence he could offer the Russians of Western support for the great offensives in the East'.[18] He met with Sinclair, the Air Minister, on 25 January and later clarified that he had 'asked whether Berlin, and no doubt other large cities in East Germany, should not now be considered especially attractive targets'.[19] And then he had travelled to Yalta where, on the first day of the conference, the Soviets requested that the Western Allies launch air attacks on German communications in the east to cause further confusion to the already retreating German forces. By 6 February Portal, the Service Chief for Air, had instructed Bomber Command that the Chiefs of Staff had approved such attacks. The raid on Dresden began on 13 February, followed by raids on Chemnitz on 14 February and Berlin on 24 February.

Dresden had been on the target list of Bomber Command for some time: this latest instruction simply provided an added impetus to select it as a priority. The choices of target and date of attack were made by Harris on a daily basis. He would assess weather conditions before making a final decision about that night's flying. So it was Harris who selected Dresden for attack that night, but Churchill who had undoubtedly approved the principle. But when news of the raid became public and disapproval and shock were expressed, Churchill did what he could to distance himself from his responsibility.

American news reports were the first to carry information of the raids over Dresden, and their statement that the raid proved that the Allied Air Chiefs were carrying out deliberate terror bombings caused great upset. These news reports were suppressed in Britain, but awkward questions were asked in the House of Commons that were reported. Realising that the reactions to Dresden represented a shift in public opinion – from an acceptance that bombing German cities (and people) was justified when British cities were being attacked by German bombers to a realisation that bombing now seemed unjustified with German defeat being a certainty – Churchill composed a note to the Chiefs of Staff. He wrote: 'It seems to me that the moment has come when the question of bombing of German cities simply for the sake of increasing the terror . . . should be reviewed . . . The destruction of Dresden remains a serious query against the conduct of Allied bombing.'[20] One historian has written that, 'It is impossible to regard this memorandum as anything other than a calculated political attempt by the Prime Minister to distance himself from the bombing of Dresden.'[21] Whether true or not, he was persuaded by Portal to rewrite the memo in less emotional and inflammatory tones, since the original had caused a great deal of bad feeling among the Air Staff whom Churchill had condemned for carrying out the strategy he himself had approved.

Rather like the debate over whether or not to bomb Auschwitz, the Dresden raid raised uncomfortable questions about Allied bombing. It was claimed publicly that all bombing raids were carried out against targets that were primarily military or industrial, and were not intended to result in large civilian casualty figures. Internal policy documents were more honest. An Air Ministry directive of February 1942 'was the blueprint for the attack on Germany's cities' in stating that raids would target German industry but would also aim at the harassment of the civilian population.[22] By July 1944 the Chiefs of Staff were minuting Churchill that 'the time might well come in the not too distant future when an all-out attack by every means at our disposal on German civilian morale might be decisive'.[23] But the British could not admit that civilians were being targeted for several reasons. Not least was the fourth Hague Convention of 1907 which had outlawed the aerial bombardment of civilians. The Allies, too, were determined to be seen as morally superior to Nazi Germany. Admitting to a policy of killing unarmed civilians would have undermined this stance.

Churchill was perfectly well aware that the policy of area bombing, of which he had been a powerful if inconsistent proponent, 'may not have been sound strategy, [and] was certainly not fair play'.[24] He also knew that had Britain not been part of the alliance of countries that won the Second World War, he and his fellow colleagues would have been condemned as war criminals, with bombing of cities cited as one of their most serious war crimes. Commander Harris was not awarded a peerage at the end of the war, possibly because the morality of his campaign was not clear cut and, therefore, could not be publicly rewarded. Churchill's belated offer of a baronetcy to him in the 1950s was perhaps a recognition that there had seemed to be little alternative to bombing as a key policy, moral doubts or not. Probably for these reasons he was reluctant to talk of Dresden, to the point of being deliberately misleading, as the following story illustrates. 'As for the carnage at Dresden, its details seemed to have slipped Churchill's memory . . . when asked by an historian after the war to verify some data about the incident, he replied: "I cannot recall anything about it. I thought the Americans did it."'[25]

Questions

1. Why has the bombing of Dresden become such a controversial issue in British historiography?
2. To what extent do you agree with the statement that 'The Allies' strategic bombing offensive made no significant contribution to the defeat of Nazi Germany'?

SOURCES

1. THE DEBATE OVER WHETHER TO BOMB AUSCHWITZ

Source A: letter from Anthony Eden, Foreign Secretary, to Archibald Sinclair, Minister for Air, 7 July 1944

You will remember that I referred in the House last Wednesday to the appalling persecution of Jews in Hungary. On July 6th Weizmann, of the Jewish Agency for Palestine, came to see me with further information about it which had reached the Agency's representatives in Istanbul, Geneva and Lisbon, the main point of which was that, according to these reports, 400,000 Hungarian Jews had already been deported to what he called the 'death camps' at Birkenau in Upper Silesia, where there are four crematoriums with a gassing and burning capacity of 60,000 a day and where, incidentally, in the course of the last year, over one and a half million Jews from all over Europe are reported to have been killed.

Dr Weizmann admitted that there seemed little enough that we could do to stop these horrors, but he suggested that something might be done to stop the operation of the death camps by

(1) bombing the railway lines leading to Birkenau (and to any other similar camps if we get to hear of them); and
(2) bombing the camps themselves with the object of destroying the plant used for gassing and burning.

I should add that I told Weizmann that, as you may know, we had already considered suggestion (1) above but that I would re-examine it and also the further suggestion of bombing the camps themselves.

Could you let me know how the Air Ministry view the feasibility of these proposals? I very much hope that it will be possible to do something. I have the authority of the Prime Minister to say that he agrees.

Source B: minute from Sinclair to Eden, 15 July 1944

I entirely agree that it is our duty to consider every possible plan that might help, and I have, therefore, examined:

a) interrupting the railways
b) destroying the plant
c) other interference with the camps.

I am informed that (a) is out of our power. It is only by an enormous concentration of our bomber forces that we have been able to interrupt communications in Normandy; the distance of Silesia from our bases entirely rules out our doing anything of the kind.

Bombing the plant is out of the bounds of possibility for Bomber Command, because the distance is too great for the attack to be carried out at night. It might be carried out by the Americans by daylight but it would be a costly and hazardous operation. It might be ineffective, and, even if the plant was destroyed, I am not clear that it would really help the victims.

There is just one possibility, and that is bombing the camps, and possibly dropping weapons at the same time, in the hope that some of the victims may be able to escape. We did something of the kind in France, when we made a breach in the walls of a prison camp and we think that 150 men who had been condemned to death managed to escape.

Source C: letter from Air Commodore Grant, the Director of Intelligence (Operations) at the Air Ministry to Victor Cavendish-Bentinck, at the Foreign Office, 13 August 1944

I am perturbed at having heard nothing more from the Foreign Office about the problem of Birkenau since . . . the 5th of this month.

You will appreciate that as the Secretary of State for Air had instructed the Air Staff to take action on Mr Eden's request, it is a matter of great urgency for me to obtain photographic cover of the camps and installations in the Birkenau area. The information at present in our possession is insufficient for a reconnaissance aircraft to have a reasonable chance of obtaining the cover required, and only the Foreign Office can obtain the information I need.

Source D: extract of text from the Holocaust Exhibition at the Imperial War Museum, 2000

Could Auschwitz have been bombed? Pros and Cons.

Bombing was inaccurate (fewer than half of all bombs dropped in 1944 came within 1,000 feet of their targets), and bombs falling on the barracks blocks could have killed thousands of prisoners who were not destined for the gas chambers. Precision raids would have required the use of Mosquito fighter-bombers at the extreme of their range, flying by bright moonlight over hundreds of miles of enemy territory.

Many former prisoners of Auschwitz say they would have welcomed bombing as a sign of moral support, even if some had been killed. The Allies did carry out raids against prisons and camps in Western Europe; for example, a Mosquito raid on the Gestapo headquarters in Copenhagen, 500 miles from base as compared to 600 for Auschwitz, allowed several hundred members of the underground resistance to escape. Weapons were also air-dropped to support the Warsaw Uprising in September 1944. The idea of dropping weapons at Auschwitz was proposed but apparently never seriously considered.

Source E: Allied air raids on the I.G. Farben synthetic oil plant at Monowitz, 1944

Date	Damage reports	Oil production
20.8.44	1,336,500lb bombs caused significant damage to synthetic oil plant, stores, sheds, offices, and huts in the labour camp	Average monthly oil production estimated at 2,000–2,750 tons
13.9.44	1,000,500lb bombs scored a direct hit but with only slight damage but injuring 300 slave workers: accidental hits on Auschwitz resulted in destruction of SS barracks and death of 15 SS, 28 SS injured; hit on clothing workshop with 40 camp inmates killed and 65 injured; and on Birkenau resulting in some damage to railway embankment and sidings, and death of 30 civilian workers	
18.12.44	Bombing hit plant and the labour camp, but reconnaissance photographs also showed repairs being made to previous damage	Production had dropped to 1,200 tons by December
20.12.44	Bombing caused heavy damage to the plant, but oil production continued: accidental hits on Birkenau resulted in the SS sick bay being damaged with 5 SS killed	
19.1.45	The last raid on Monowitz resulted in cutting all power and water supplies to Auschwitz, where only 850 sick had been abandoned by retreating Nazis: 200 of these people died before the Soviet liberation on 27 January	Production fell to 500 tons by January

Questions

1. Read Source A. Comment on the significance of Eden's reference to the deportation of the Hungarian Jews to Auschwitz. (3)
2. Read Source B. What difficulties did Sinclair identify in the proposal to bomb Auschwitz or its railway lines? (5)
3. To what extent does the evidence in Sources D and E contradict the difficulties identified in Source B? (5)

4. How does Source D support Sinclair's suggestion (in Source B) to drop weapons over the camp as being a possible alternative? (5)
5. Using these Sources and your own knowledge, assess which of the explanations given for not bombing Auschwitz is the most convincing, giving reasons for your answer. (12)

Worked answer

3. Both Sources D and E contain evidence that challenge Sinclair's assertions that bombing Auschwitz was 'out of the bounds of possibility' for reasons of distance, technical difficulty, cost and danger. Source D states that a previous raid over Copenhagen had succeeded in causing enough damage to enable prisoners to escape a Gestapo prison, despite it being 500 miles away from base (while Auschwitz was 600 miles away). Source E provides evidence that the Americans were willing to risk the hazards (and bear the costs) of bombing this far into enemy territory. The USAAF carried out five separate air raids over Monowitz, which was the factory that used labour from Auschwitz, and was situated very close by. Several of the raids resulted in accidental hits on the camp. However, this fact serves both to confirm and refute Sinclair's doubts over the possibility of bombing the camp, for while it was clearly possible, the results were not always to the benefit of the prisoners, since inmates were killed and injured by the raids of 13 September 1944 and 19 January 1945. Source D provides evidence that Sinclair's suggestion of dropping weapons over the camp could have been possible, since this was accomplished in September 1944 to help the Polish uprising in Warsaw.

2. THE DECISION TO BOMB DRESDEN

Source F: Bomber Command briefing paper on Dresden, issued to groups and squadrons on the eve of the raid

Dresden, the seventh largest city in Germany and not much smaller than Manchester, is also far the largest unbombed built-up area the enemy has got. In the midst of winter with refugees pouring westwards and troops to be rested, roofs are at a premium, not only to give shelter to workers, refugees and troops alike, but to house the administrative services displaced from other areas. At one time well known for its china, Dresden had developed into an industrial city of first-class importance, and like any large city with its multiplicity of telephone and rail facilities, is of major value for controlling the defence of that part of the front now threatened by Marshal Koniev's breakthrough.

The intentions of the attack are to hit the enemy where he will feel it most, behind an already partially collapsed front, to prevent the use of the city in the way of further advance, and incidentally to show the Russians when they arrive what Bomber Command can do.

Source G: the historian Martin Gilbert writing about the reasons for the raid on Dresden in a book published in 1993

On February 5, at a meeting of the British, American and Soviet Chiefs of Staff, the Russians pointed out that several divisions of German troops were being brought back across Europe to the Eastern Front. The Russians then asked for a substantial Allied air attack on German communications in the Berlin–Leipzig–Dresden region, and for the bombing of these three specific cities, as a matter of urgency, to prevent the German reinforcements moving eastwards against them. This was agreed to by the Anglo-American Chiefs of Staff, and instructions given for a series of Anglo-American bombing raids. Dresden was to be one of the targets.

Source H: another historian, Max Hastings, offers a different explanation in his history of Bomber Command published in 1979

Dresden had indeed been on Harris's target lists for months, but the impetus finally to launch the raid on the great East German city came from the Prime Minister and the Chief of Air Staff.
   . . . as Churchill prepared to leave for Yalta for the last major Allied conference of the European war, he turned almost impulsively to consider what evidence he could offer the Russians of Western support for their great offensives in the East. He talked to Sinclair on the night of 25 January. The next day the Air Ministry informed the Air Staff that the Prime Minister wanted to know Bomber Command's proposals for 'blasting the Germans in their retreat'.

Source I: memorandum from Churchill to Ismay and the Chiefs of Staff Committee, 28 March 1945

It seems to me that the moment has come when the question of bombing German cities simply for the sake of increasing the terror, though under other pretexts, should be reviewed. Otherwise we shall come into control of an utterly ruined land. We shall not, for instance, be able to get housing materials out of Germany for our own needs because some temporary provision would have to be made for the Germans themselves. The destruction of Dresden remains a serious query against the conduct of Allied bombing. I am of the opinion that military objectives must henceforward be more strictly studied in our own interests rather than that of the enemy.

The Foreign Secretary had spoken to me on this subject, and I feel the need for more precise concentration upon military objectives, such as oil and communications behind the immediate battle-zone, rather than on mere acts of terror and wanton destruction, however impressive.

Source J: revised memorandum from Churchill to Ismay and the Chiefs of Staff Committee, 1 April 1945

It seems to me that the moment has come when the question of the so called 'area bombing' of German cities should be reviewed from the point of view of our own interests. If we come into control of an entirely ruined land, there will be a great shortage of accommodation for ourselves and our Allies; and we shall be unable to get housing materials out of Germany for our own needs . . . We must see to it that our attacks do not do more to harm ourselves in the long run than they do to the enemy's immediate war effort. Pray let me have your views.

Questions

1. Study Source G. What reasons does this Source give for the targeting of Dresden? (3)
2. What does Source F add to the information given by Source G about the reasons for the air attack on Dresden? (5)
3. In what ways do Sources G and H disagree over how the decision to target Dresden was made? (5)
4. Examine Sources I and J. Explain why Source J was deemed to be a more acceptable version of the memorandum than Source I. (5)
5. Using your own knowledge, assess how useful these Sources are to a historian researching the reasons for the raid on Dresden in February 1945. (12)

Worked answer

5. Sources G and H are both useful to historians researching the decision to bomb Dresden, since they offer different, but not incompatible, explanations. Source H places the responsibility for the decision with Churchill, who wanted to offer the Soviets some evidence of British support for their battles on the Eastern Front when meeting them at the Yalta Conference. Source G focuses on the fact that, at Yalta, the Soviets requested more air attacks on East German cities and communications. These two episodes were within days of each other and it seems possible that the Soviet request served to reinforce Churchill's own idea, and to give the operation greater urgency. Source F offers a different type of

evidence in that it is the text of Bomber Command's briefing note, and is concerned, therefore, with strategic reasons for targeting the city, not political motives, as in Sources G and H. The briefing document would have been a secret document, produced for operational purposes and not for public consumption. For this reason it is possible to assume that it contains an honest assessment of the value of targeting and damaging Dresden. The briefing gives a number of strategic reasons: that the city was the 'seventh largest city in Germany', a centre of industry, communications and transport networks, which would all have been important for Germany's war effort. It also identifies that the city had become a centre for refugees and 'administrative services' that had been displaced by the Soviet advance. In identifying these so clearly the document reveals that one of the major aims of any raids over the city was to add to the chaos of a region already in disarray, 'to hit the enemy where he will feel it most'. It is also implied that any raid over the city was going to result in the death and injury of many civilians – including a large number of refugees. Churchill's two memoranda (Sources I and J) are valuable in that the first document reveals the extent to which it was accepted among military leaders that air attacks such as that over Dresden, were designed to cause 'terror and wanton destruction'. The fact that Churchill was persuaded to censor his own candid comments to produce a less controversial memo tells historians that the British were uncomfortable with admitting that this was a primary aim of their bombing campaign and wished to tone down any references made to it. Taken together, the Sources provide a useful range of evidence of political and military origin. They are also useful in identifying the unease with which the Air Ministry viewed its actions in aiming to reduce German morale by targeting civilians.

8

<u>ELDER, 1945–1955</u>

BACKGROUND NARRATIVE

'The decision of the British people has been recorded in the votes counted to-day. I have therefore laid down the charge which was placed upon me in darker times.'[1]

Churchill was greatly shocked by the result of the general election and his immediate response was to take an extended holiday abroad, perhaps less to recover his health and more to recover his wounded pride. As leader of the opposition he presided over some far-reaching reforms of his party but, as usual, preferred to leave the domestic chores to others and to concentrate on international affairs. His reputation as the most famous Englishman meant he was a popular speaker in Europe and the USA, and made a number of significant speeches on the theme of international affairs, including his description of the 'iron curtain'. He spent much less time in the House of Commons, which created a vacuum in the Tory leadership until Butler, Eden and Macmillan took it upon themselves to fill the gap.

Churchill won his first general election to become Prime Minister in October 1951 at the age of seventy-six. With the succession of the new Queen in 1952 there was much optimism and talk of a new Elizabethan Age. But there was also an acknowledgement that this was Churchill's swansong and few expected him to see out the full Parliament as Prime Minister. His fitness for office and relationship with his successor were important issues from the beginning of his administration, and became more so as the years went by. The subject of his retirement was raised almost as soon as he had returned to Number 10. Partly this was because he repeatedly promised to retire but postponed the date, and partly because of his failing health. He suffered a serious stroke in June 1953 that nearly killed him. At the time only a very small number of people knew and, incredibly, they kept it secret from the public and the press. Churchill was incapacitated for several months. Butler was left in charge of the Cabinet since Eden, too, was unwell, recovering from a botched operation. Churchill decided to retire but again postponed it after making a dramatic recovery in time to deliver a great speech to the party conference that October. But the stroke had taken its toll and 'it proved impossible to arrest his physical and mental decline. The human dynamo was simply running down.'[2] To Eden's lasting frustration, it was April 1955 before the old man retired.

ANALYSIS (1): ASSESS CHURCHILL'S RECORD AS PRIME MINISTER 1951–1955

Churchill's second premiership is usually described as a 'quiet administration' during which the ideological differences between Conservative and Labour reduced. The term 'Butskellism' was coined during these years to describe the political consensus that seemed to dominate domestic policies, such as the commitment to full employment and support for social and welfare services. However, there were high expectations for Churchill's new government: of dismantling the remaining restrictions of wartime Britain, and of leading the country into an economic and international revival.

That the Conservatives were returned to government with a majority of only seventeen would have limited attempts to introduce radical policies had Churchill been bent on a wholesale undoing of Labour's post-war achievements. But from the outset such radicalism looked unlikely. In forming his administration Churchill chose to work with men he had known from his wartime government, and had hoped to re-form a coalition – with the Liberals. This latter wish did not happen but 'his constant yearning for coalition politics and his image of himself as a national leader rising above partisan political calculations'[3] clearly still dominated his thinking. In his first speech to Parliament he promised 'several years of quiet steady administration, if only to allow Socialist legislation to reach its full fruition'.[4] The historian Addison has described it as 'a Government of Tory wets, for whom social harmony was a higher priority than economic efficiency'.[5]

The only piece of major Labour legislation that Churchill insisted on undoing was the nationalisation of the iron and steel and road-haulage industries. Denationalising iron and steel proved more complicated than he had imagined. It took until May 1953 to restore it to private ownership and another ten years to complete the sale of its assets, by which time Labour had returned to power to renationalise it. There had been promises of a reorganisation of the publicly owned industries, but an inquiry into the coal industry was quietly shelved and no such reorganisation took place under Churchill. Similarly the organisation of and expenditure on the welfare state followed on from Labour. Three official studies, on national insurance, pensions and the National Health Service, resulted in no changes being made despite there being obvious issues to address. Instead, government spending on social services increased from 39.2 per cent of total spending in 1951 to 43 per cent in 1955 and prescription charges were increased to meet rising costs.

Two more active areas of domestic policy were the result of more traditional Conservative thought. The first such success was in housing. This had been the most definite electoral promise – to build 300,000 new houses a year. In appointing Macmillan, Churchill ensured that housing was led by an imaginative minister who applied Conservative thinking to the problem and encouraged local authorities to allow more private contractors to build public housing. This dramatically increased the construction rate so that, in 1953, 327,000 new houses were built, and in 1954, 354,000. Churchill's role, aside from recognising Macmillan's talent, was actively to support him in his struggles with the Treasury for the necessary funding. Churchill's concern for people's everyday comforts, evident in his wartime leadership, was still important to him. It was the reason behind his determination to dismantle the remaining wartime controls – rationing in particular. He had never liked rationing and was keen to end it as soon as possible. Because of the economic difficulties of the early years of his administration it was July 1954 before the last foods (bacon and other meat) were taken off the ration. Nevertheless, 'The Churchill Government dismantled economic controls at a much faster rate than Labour would have done.'[6] Yet these years saw an acceptance by many Conservatives of the necessity for some measure of state control of the economy.

In part this acceptance came out of necessity. At the first Cabinet meeting of this administration, the Treasury revealed that Britain's balance of payments deficit was much larger than expected and that by 1952 the debt could not be met from reserves. Initially this forced the Cabinet to increase, not decrease, a number of economic controls – reducing the meat ration, cutting imports, the tourist rate and public spending in education. Churchill also insisted that all senior ministers, including himself, take a pay cut. It was during this period of austerity that a revolutionary plan was contemplated. Named 'Operation Robot', it was a proposal to make sterling convertible and to float it on the world money markets, allowing it to find its value against other currencies. It would have fallen in value, thereby bringing imports and exports back into balance. However, it would have caused an uncomfortable and unpopular rise in unemployment and prices and so was rejected. For some historians, like Keith Middlemass, the failure to adopt 'Robot' was a lost opportunity to restructure the economy and place it in a stronger position to cope with the changes that were to come in the next decades.

Churchill himself recommended that 'Robot' be rejected because it would be too divisive, and so the Cabinet chose more orthodox means of trying to control the economy. Thus the Chancellor, R. A. Butler, raised the bank rate to reduce consumer demand and applied the first 'stop' of the 'stop–go' economics of the 1950s. By 1953–1954 the Conservatives were claiming success. The Stock Exchange was booming and the standard of living had risen. The government decided to withdraw from the Marshall Plan a year early. But the recovery was due more to favourable changes in the terms of trade than to Butler's policies and did not last much beyond 1955. In his determination to avoid industrial confrontation Churchill conceded a number of wage claims that had inflationary consequences. This 'policy of industrial appeasement has been strongly criticised as one more example of the failure to develop a strategy for the modernisation of British industry after the war'.[7]

So it seems that domestic policy was not very innovative despite – or perhaps because of – Churchill's one attempt at innovation. Drawing up his first peacetime Cabinet, he attempted to keep it small by appointing 'overlords', each one to oversee a collection of departments and represent them at Cabinet meetings. Thus Lord Leathers became Overlord of the Ministries of Transport, Fuel and Power; Lord Woolton of Food and Agriculture; and Lord Cherwell of Scientific Research and the Prime Minister's Statistical Section. 'In itself the system had a lot to recommend it. The trouble was that the "overlords" all sat in the House of Lords and this made procedure difficult.'[8] It meant that the Commons could not question the overlords themselves, only their junior ministers, and many MPs believed this was unconstitutional. Moreover, the experiment did not result in improved coordination, but in a more confused chain of command. Churchill reviewed the experiment in August 1953 and found it was easy to abandon since none of the overlords had created anything of substance. But it was, perhaps, not an inconsequential experiment. The idea of merging ministries to streamline an increasingly complex system of government lived on. Agriculture, Fisheries and Food continued as an integrated ministry and in 1964 the individual service ministries were merged to form the Ministry of Defence.

In matters of defence and foreign affairs Churchill's administration saw more far-reaching changes. With the successful testing of the atomic bomb in October 1952, Churchill became Britain's first nuclear Prime Minister. This had mixed implications. On the one hand, 'Diplomatically, it seemed to put (or help keep) Great Britain on the same level as the USA and the USSR,'[9] but on the other, it allowed Britain artificially to preserve her diplomatic status and to discourage a thorough review of her overseas and international obligations. The Global Strategy paper of 1952 acknowledged the gap between Britain's economic resources and her overseas commitments and recommended a shift to nuclear deterrence as the cheapest way of maintaining them. It was argued that nuclear weaponry was going to cost less than conventional armed forces. Churchill's Cabinet took the decision to go ahead with developing a hydrogen bomb in 1952, making it public in the Defence White Paper of March 1955. Being an atomic power set Britain apart from other European states and forced the USA to continue to treat Britain as a partner, so preserving the 'special relationship'. But this became an expensive way to maintain status, since the USA expected Britain to contribute more to European defence than any other European state. Perhaps 'building up the British economy would in the long run have done more for Britain's position in the world than did the bomb',[10] but Churchill was determined that Britain would be more than just one of many European powers.

His determination to forge a close relationship with the USA had enabled Britain to survive the Second World War and he was set on building closer relations with the Presidency once he was back in office. He found it harder than imagined to do so, with both Truman and his successor Eisenhower. Tensions arose over the Korean War (when Churchill was afraid of American willingness to use the atomic bomb), war in Indo-China (Vietnam) and European security. In the changed circumstances of the Cold War Britain had found the USA to be more tolerant of her imperial authority in such regions as Iran and Egypt because it was seen to be a barrier to the spread of communism. But the price of this was that Britain was expected to play a greater role in the politics of Europe. This was difficult for Churchill because 'Despite his earlier speeches on the theme of European unity – and in particular his call for the creation of a European army – Churchill had never thought in terms of Britain herself forming part of a united Europe.'[11] His statement of November 1951 that Britain would not join the European Defence Community (EDC) shocked European federalists, but following the French refusal to ratify the EDC and growing pressure from the USA to rescue the initiative, Churchill's government was bounced into a deeper involvement.

Eden embarked on a diplomatic offensive that led to the creation of the Western European Union in October 1954. Significantly it was Britain's commitment of forces to Europe that secured its creation. Eden's success in chairing the Geneva Conference throughout the summer of 1954 (which ended the war in Indo-China) and the partial resolution of difficulties in Egypt and Iran all served to create the impression of a successful foreign policy. However, Churchill was unable to realise his ambition to organise a summit of leaders despite the amount of time and attention he gave to this task in the later years of his leadership. And Eden found that his settlements in the Middle East were not as robust as he thought. Indeed, the failure of Churchill's government to review Britain's imperial commitments or outlook (unsurprising given his personal attachment to the British Empire) was a serious flaw.

After his stroke in June 1953 Churchill found he could concentrate on fewer issues and practically abandoned domestic policies in pursuit of a summit with the Soviets. 'Often it seemed as if the scope and pace of peacetime government as a whole was quite beyond him.'[12] Addison argues that until the stroke 'Churchill was a comparatively effective Prime Minister'[13] who led 'a more patrician style of government with a minimum of propaganda and public relations'[14] that was an interlude between the socialism of the post-war Labour government and the consumerism of the Conservative governments of the later 1950s and 1960s. Opportunities to effect real change – in Britain's foreign relations, and in her economic policy – were rejected in favour of less divisive options so as to secure a 'quiet administration' for Churchill's last years in power. What it did not secure was a quiet future for Britain, and nor did Churchill ensure that his successor, Eden, was adequate to the challenges that faced him when he became Prime Minister in April 1955.

Questions

1. How was Churchill able to remain as Prime Minister until 1955?

2. To what extent did Churchill's government of 1951–1955 lay the foundations for Conservative survival in power until 1964?

ANALYSIS (2): IN WHAT WAYS AND FOR WHAT REASONS DID CHURCHILL SEEK TO INFLUENCE INTERNATIONAL RELATIONS IN THE YEARS 1946 TO 1955?

Until 1951 Churchill was in opposition. His defeat at the polls in 1945 stripped him of the wide-ranging powers to which he had become accustomed during the war. However, he embarked on a career as an international statesman, speaking at venues in Europe and the USA. 'Of course, he had no official standing, but his massive reputation allowed him to intervene with an authority denied to others.'[15] Until about 1950 he campaigned consistently to force the Soviets to renegotiate the European settlement that he had helped to shape, and although lacking office, he proved he still had influence over international affairs. A number of his speeches proved significant and, some historians have argued, decisive to the course of the early Cold War. His views changed dramatically during 1949–1950 however, and he became an early advocate of détente. Once elected Prime Minister in 1951 he had far more authority as Britain's leader, but found it difficult to convert Truman or Eisenhower to his idea of a summit with the Soviets. His last years in power saw a decline in the amount of influence he could wield, even though it was by then the sole focus of his efforts.

It seems ironic that Churchill spent the early post-war years intent on changing the European settlement of which he had been an architect, at the wartime conferences of Teheran, Yalta and Potsdam. Yet this was the motivation behind his calls to confront the USSR. Having given in to Stalin's demands for control over Poland at Yalta, and having failed, in 1945, to persuade the Americans to push on and occupy as much German territory as possible before the Soviets arrived, he was dissatisfied with the borders thus established. He did not believe that they were the basis for a long-term peace. Comparing them to the borders established by the short-lived Versailles settlement after the First World War, he was pessimistic: 'In those days there were high hopes and unbounded confidence that wars were over . . . I do not see or feel that same confidence or even the same hopes in the haggard world at the present time.'[16] But his determination to confront the Soviets and demand a renegotiation of the settlement was unwelcome to both British and American governments. During 1945 and early 1946 they were unwilling to take such a course of action, believing that they were in too weak a position to make demands that they believed Stalin was sure to reject.

All this was to change, beginning with the delivery of Churchill's most famous post-war speech at Fulton, Missouri, on 5 March 1946. In it he coined the phrase 'iron curtain' to describe the division of Europe between the liberal West and communist East. 'Churchill stormed Western public opinion on behalf of the Cold War. It was a task eminently suited to his unique talents.'[17] Initial responses to the speech were unfavourable. His condemnation of Soviet conduct in Eastern Europe and blunt statement that 'this is certainly not the Liberated Europe we fought to build up. Nor is it one which contains the essentials of permanent peace'[18] were greeted with shock and dismay. How was it possible for him to criticise his former wartime ally in this way? 'Is it that he was still at heart the same fanatical enemy of Marxism–Leninism that he had been when the Soviet Union was created'[19] and had reverted to his old warmongering self? Or did he genuinely fear that 'the indefinite expansion of their power and doctrines'[20] was threatening to destabilise the world enough to be risking another war? Once again he had caused a stir by voicing concerns that others had dared not. But his position was not so isolated as it first appeared.

A number of historians now agree that this speech was used to test out public (and Soviet) reaction to a harder-line policy. In stating, 'I am convinced that there is nothing [the Soviet Union] admires so much as strength and nothing for which they have less respect than weakness,'[21] Churchill was voicing not just his own opinion but that of Truman and his Secretary of State, Byrnes. From mid-February 1946 onwards they had begun to pursue a more robust course of action with the Soviets, issuing a string of formal complaints about Soviet non-cooperation in a number of key regions, from Austria to Iran. Churchill's appearance at Fulton seemed an excellent chance to 'bring this new militancy from the shadows of diplomacy into the open arena of American public politics'.[22] He had the right reputation to deliver this message from his pre-war warnings about Nazi Germany and his inspirational wartime speeches. If he could not storm public opinion on behalf of Truman's new policy, who could? The extent of their complicity is shown by the fact of their travelling together to Fulton by train, a two-day journey during which they discussed the ideas that formed the basis of Churchill's speech and he made last-minute adjustments to it, including the addition of the 'iron curtain' passage.

Within days of its delivery, Soviet actions in Iran seemed to prove Churchill's assertion that 'What they desire [are] the fruits of war and the indefinite expansion of their power'.[23] With a concrete issue on which to focus – Soviet refusal to withdraw troops from Iran in contravention of their wartime agreement with the British to do so – public opinion in the USA began to move in favour of a firmer, less accommodating policy. Evidence for this is provided by the results of two opinion polls that asked about the least popular element of Churchill's speech: the formation of an Anglo-American alliance. He had asked that the USA and Britain and the Commonwealth form 'a fraternal association of the English-speaking peoples' to ensure the 'prevention of war [and] the continuous rise of world organization'.[24] Days after the speech only 18 per cent of Americans were in favour of this idea. A month later this figure had risen to 85 per cent.[25] The speech also had consequences for relations with the Soviet Union. Stalin found himself in a very difficult position because of it. Churchill had raised a challenge to him, yet Stalin found he was condemned whether he pulled back from confrontation in Iran (in which case he would prove Churchill's claim that the USSR responded only to force) or if he stayed put, and proved right Churchill's accusation that the Soviets were expansionist. He was also livid at the comment that the American monopoly of the atomic bomb was 'God willed'. As a result, the Soviets became even less cooperative, and the posturing of 1945–1946 hardened into the battle lines of the Cold War.[26]

Thus 'widely credited with inaugurating the Cold War' Churchill was nevertheless without real power. Attlee was Britain's Prime Minister (and was far less hard line) and all Churchill could do to influence matters was to continue to deliver speeches in public and engineer private meetings and correspondence with Truman. But following his 'iron curtain' speech, his and Truman's views began to diverge. While Truman and Byrnes developed a policy of 'containment' by which Soviet expansion into any key region was to be resisted by American resources, Churchill urged a different approach. 'Churchill supported containment, but for him it was never an end in itself. Unwilling to wait passively for the collapse of communism, he sought to shape history rather than to rely on it to do his work for him. What he was after was a negotiated settlement.'[27] He saw America's monopoly of nuclear weapons as the most powerful bargaining chip with which to demand concessions from the USSR, whereas others, Truman and Attlee included, were more reticent. But for Churchill there was a real urgency to take advantage while the West still had this monopoly, for it would surely not be long before the Soviet Union would develop its own bomb. He explained his position to the Conservative Party Conference in 1948:

Nothing stands between Europe today and complete subjugation to Communist tyranny but the atomic bomb in American possession . . .

What do you suppose would be the position this afternoon if it had been Communist Russia instead of free enterprise America which had created the atomic weapon? . . . No one in his sense can believe that we have a limitless period of time before us. We ought to bring matters to a head and make a final settlement.[28]

Such confrontational talk was rejected by both Truman and Attlee. It seemed unthinkable to run the risk of actual military conflict when tensions were already so high. The Soviet blockade of Berlin and unscrupulous elimination of political opponents in Eastern Europe persuaded the Western leaders to concentrate on building political and economic unity there, not challenging the wartime settlement.

Churchill had views on this, too, although they were not without controversy, of course. While the Truman and Attlee administrations struggled to accept the need for greater involvement in the movement towards European unity, Churchill was able to declare himself a supporter of a 'United States of Europe'. During a speech in Zurich in September 1946 he declared: 'We must build a kind of United States of Europe . . . the first step . . . must be a partnership between France and Germany.'[29] In advocating this reorganisation of Europe, Churchill was not showing himself to be a federalist, nor was he recommending that Britain be integral to this organisation. 'His instinct was that Britain should remain outside any European organisation.'[30] But he was supportive of it. Although he suggested that the organisation could be political as well as economic and military, his aim was more 'a matter of creating an atmosphere, a mood which would enable the governments of these separate states to reach agreement and avoid the horrible penalties of war'.[31] He saw this European organisation working alongside the UN and the special relationship between Britain and the USA to preserve peace.

Churchill's speech at Zurich was full of characteristically vivid language, but in describing the 'vast quivering mass of tormented, hungry, care-worn and bewildered human beings [who] gape at the ruins of their cities and homes',[32] he focused American thinking on the vulnerability of a ruined Europe to communist expansionism. In a press conference to announce the plan for the economic recovery of Europe in June 1947, General Marshall revealed that Churchill's speech had inspired him to formulate the scheme. Furthermore, Churchill's calls for a 'Council of Europe' that would give political unity to the region were realised when such a council was established in August 1948. With the creation of the Brussels Pact (March 1948) and NATO (April 1949), Churchill's trio of economic, military and political pan-European organisations had been created. He was not responsible for these events – he was without real power to implement such acts – but he was able to believe with some justification that his influence had been significant in their development.

When, in October 1951, Churchill was returned to power, there were high hopes in Britain and Europe that his influence would be all the greater in foreign affairs. By this time, though, the world scene was even more complex: the Korean War had broken out, the USA was no longer the only nuclear power and the Presidency was to change hands shortly. All these elements affected Churchill's prosecution of foreign affairs. By 1950 he had begun to advocate not confrontation but conciliation, through a high-level summit with the Soviet leaders, 'to enable us at least to live peacefully together'.[33] It was 'a revolutionary idea at that stage of the Cold War'.[34] 'He had no specific agenda in view; what he apparently wanted was to take part in an unstructured but spectacular meeting of world leaders which would somehow produce a general easement.'[35] Put this way it seems a woolly idea but this concept of 'peaceful coexistence to permit the erosion of time' – détente – became an important element of the Cold War until the 1980s.

In the early 1950s, however, Truman was not persuaded and resisted Churchill's attempts. Even the arrival of Stalin's 'peace note' of 10 March 1952 could not change his mind. Whether this proposal for talks was genuine was never discovered. It must have been very frustrating for Churchill that he could not act without American support, but Britain was much reduced compared to her wartime role, and Churchill could only do his best to persuade and cajole both Truman and then Eisenhower to his policy of détente.

Churchill had several reasons for his about-turn in foreign policy. He undoubtedly saw himself as uniquely qualified to deal with the Soviets, based on his wartime experiences, and he certainly expected to play a leading role in any such summit. Indeed, there is a suspicion that his desire to participate in a 'spectacular meeting of world leaders' is what kept him in office far beyond his age and energy allowed. Carlton goes as far as arguing that Churchill 'allowed this consideration to distort almost all his thinking about the Soviet Union and he unscrupulously attempted to manipulate other world leaders to serve his essentially selfish purposes'.[36] However, there were a number of less personal reasons for Churchill to pursue détente.

In August 1949 the USA lost the monopoly of atomic weapons when the USSR successfully detonated its own nuclear bomb. The position of strength that Churchill had so relied on as the basis for his prior policy of confronting the Soviets had been removed. Between this point and

October 1952, when she successfully detonated an atomic bomb of her own, Britain was the only one of the wartime Big Three that did not have a nuclear capability. Not only was Britain's status much reduced in comparison to the two superpowers, but 'Western European cities, including London, had become vulnerable to Soviet atomic strikes'.[37] Unable, then, to risk confrontation, the alternative for Churchill's Britain was to opt for détente. His repeated attempts to arrange a summit between the Soviets, Americans and British came to nothing.

Questions

1. In what ways did the foreign policies of Churchill's government differ from those of the Labour governments of 1945–1951?
2. What role did Churchill play in the development and maintenance of the 'special relationship' between Britain and the USA?

SOURCES

1. WAS CHURCHILL FIT FOR OFFICE?

Source A: two historians have written this in their history of the Conservative Party, published in 1979

Churchill was nearly seventy-seven when he formed his peace-time Government. He was thus the oldest Prime Minister since Gladstone. There was no doubt that he was long past his peak, but he still towered above any possible rivals in terms of prestige, personality and experience of government. He was still able to dominate the House of Commons, and he carried weight, internationally, out of all proportion to the resources of the country which he governed. Age was certainly taking its toll, but there was as yet no doubt about his ability to control the Government effectively.

Source B: extracts from the diary of Churchill's private secretary, John Colville

Sunday, November 9th [1952]
He (W.) is getting tired and visibly ageing. He finds it hard work to compose a speech and ideas no longer flow. He has made two strangely simple errors in the H. of C. lately, and even when addressing the Harrow boys in Speech Room last Friday what he said dragged and lacked fire. But he has had a tiring week, with speeches, important Cabinet decisions, etc., so that I may be unduly alarmist.

Saturday, January 3rd [1953]
After dinner, in the Verandah Grill, I was left alone with the PM and fired at him about thirty questions which he might be asked at his press conference on arrival in New York. He scintillated in his replies, e.g.:

Qn: What are your views, Mr Churchill, on the present stalemate in Korea?
Ans: Better a stalemate than a checkmate.

Friday, August 14th – Saturday, August 15th and Monday, August 17th [1953]
At Chartwell. PM coming round towards resignation in October. Says he no longer has the zest for work and finds the world in an abominable state wherever he looks.

October 1953
On October 9th I went to Margate with W. for the Conservative Conference. He made a big speech the following day and did it with complete success. He had been nervous of the ordeal: his first public appearance since his stroke and a fifty-minute speech at that; but personally I had no fears as he always rises to occasions. In the event, one could see but little difference, as far as his oratory went, since before his illness.

Source C: Lord Normanbrook, Secretary to the War Cabinet, writing in 1968

For many years it had been said, by friends as well as critics, that he would not be a great peacetime Prime Minister. The special qualities which had made him an ideal national leader in war were not required in time of peace ... The problems of peacetime government did not engage his interest to the same extent as the problems of military strategy to which he had devoted himself during the war. He still followed his earlier practice of concentrating his main interest on two or three questions at a time, but his instinct in selecting the most important issues was less sure in the context of peacetime politics than it had been in war. Nor had he quite the same zest to pursue them to conclusion ... [After his stroke] the position was different. Then he was engaged in a struggle for survival – initially a struggle to preserve his life and thereafter a struggle to remain in office. It may be that, if Anthony Eden had been available when the blow first fell, Churchill would have been willing to hand over to him the reins of government ... As time went on, he found it increasingly difficult to put forth the energy required.

Source D: controversially, Churchill's doctor, Lord Moran, published extracts from his diary in 1966

November 30, 1954
Winston Churchill is eighty years of age today – a remarkable achievement for a man of his habits ... To account for his survival it is generally supposed that he has

a wonderful constitution ... On the other hand, he is often in the hands of the doctor. It is now fifteen years since I first saw him, and in that time he has had:

(i) a heart attack in Washington just after Pearl Harbour;
(ii) three attacks of pneumonia, one of which at any rate was a 'damned nice thing';
(iii) two strokes, in 1949 and 1953;
(iv) two operations, one of which found the abdomen full of adhesions and lasted two hours;
(v) senile pruritis, perhaps the most intractable of all skin troubles;
(vi) a form of conjunctivitis unlikely to clear up without a small operation.

... To this catalogue of woe I should add that for ten years he has not had a natural sleep apart from sedatives.

Source E: Roy Jenkins, a politician and historian, writing in a biography of Churchill published in 2001

Did Churchill's limpet-like attitude to the surrender of office harm his reputation or his future health and happiness? It would no doubt have been better if he had retired in 1953. The first two years of his second government were a considerable success and played a constructive role in the acceptance by the conservative half of Britain that in the post-war world the clock could not be put back to the 1930s. After that little was accomplished which, as summitry proved a wild-goose chase, could not have been done by others. But the fault lay with Eden's illness and with Butler's lack of ruthless thrust. There was no-one to push Churchill out.

Questions

1. What qualities does Source A identify as recommending Churchill for the job of Prime Minister in 1951? (3)
2. What evidence do Sources B and D offer that contradicts this recommendation? (5)
3. Discuss which of the Sources B, C or D is most useful to historians today in assessing Churchill's fitness for office. (5)
4. What other explanations does Source C offer for the 'quiet' nature of Churchill's last government? (5)
5. 'Until the stroke he suffered in June 1953 Churchill was a comparatively effective Prime Minister.' Using these Sources and your own knowledge, discuss the validity of this statement. (12)

Worked answer

2. To his diary (Source B), Colville confided his fears that Churchill was 'getting tired and visibly ageing', making 'strangely simple errors' and finding it more difficult to think clearly. To this evidence of his ageing, Colville also added his observation that Churchill was showing less of the bullish optimism that had been so characteristic of his past self, declaring, 'the world in an abominable state' and finding that he 'no longer has the zest for work'. Source D, the diary of Churchill's personal doctor, Moran, supports Colville's assertions of Churchill's physical decline. In this entry for November 1954 Moran listed the medical emergencies and illnesses that Churchill had suffered during the previous fifteen years, which included the life-threatening stroke of 1953. While Source A focuses on Churchill's political authority and experience as being important qualifications for being Prime Minister, Sources B and D offer evidence of his physical decline, and even frailty.

2. CHURCHILL AS INTERNATIONAL STATESMAN

Source F: 'Sinews of Peace' speech given by Churchill at Fulton, Missouri, 5 March 1946

A shadow has fallen upon the scenes so lately lighted by the Allied victory. Nobody knows what Soviet Russia and its communist international organisation intends to do in the immediate future, or what are the limits, if any, to their expansive and proselytising tendencies.

... From Stettin in the Baltic to Trieste in the Adriatic, an iron curtain has descended across the continent. Behind that line lie all the capitals of the ancient states of Central and Eastern Europe. Warsaw, Berlin, Prague, Vienna, Budapest, Belgrade, Bucharest and Sofia, all these famous cities and the populations around them lie in what I must call the Soviet sphere, and all are subject in one form or another not only to Soviet influence but a very high and, in many cases, increasing measure of control from Moscow ... Police governments are prevailing in nearly every case, and so far, except Czechoslovakia, there is no true democracy.

... If now the Soviet government tries, by separate action, to build up a pro-communist Germany in their areas, this will cause new, serious difficulties in the British and American zones, and will give the defeated Germans the power of putting themselves up to auction between the Soviets and the Western democracies. Whatever conclusions may be drawn from these facts – and facts they are – this is certainly not the liberated Europe we fought to build up. Nor is it one which contains the essentials of peace.

Source G: 'Sinews of Peace' speech given by Churchill at Fulton, Missouri, 5 March 1946

Now ... I come to the crux of what I have travelled here to say. Neither the sure prevention of war nor the continuous rise of world organisation will be gained without what I have called the fraternal association of the English-speaking peoples. This means a special relationship between the British Commonwealth and Empire and the United States. This is no time for generalities, and I will venture to be precise. Fraternal association requires not only the growing friendship and mutual understanding between our two vast but kindred systems of society, but the continuance of the intimate relationship between our military advisers ... It should carry with it the continuance of the present facilities for mutual security by the joint use of all naval and air force bases in the possession of either country all over the world.

Eventually there may come – I feel eventually there will come – the principle of common citizenship.

Source H: speech given by Churchill at the University of Zurich, 19 September 1946

I wish to speak to you today about the tragedy of Europe ... Over wide areas a vast quivering mass of tormented, hungry, care-worn and bewildered human beings gape at the ruins of their cities and homes, and scan the dark horizons for the approach of some new peril, tyranny or terror ... Yet all the while there is a remedy ... It is to recreate the European family, or as much of it as we can, and provide it with a structure under which it can dwell in peace, safety and in freedom ... We all know that the two world wars through which we have passed arose out of the vain passion of a newly united Germany to play the dominating part in the world ... The guilty must be punished. Germany must be deprived of the power to rearm and make another aggressive war. But when all this has been done, as it will be done, as it is being done, there must be an end to retribution ... I am now going to say something that will astonish you. The first step in the recreation of the European family must be a partnership between France and Germany. In this way only can France recover the moral leadership of Europe. There can be no revival of Europe without a spiritually great France and a spiritually great Germany. The structure of the United States of Europe, if well and truly built, will be such as to make the material strength of a single state less important.

Source I: speech made by Churchill at the Conservative Party Conference, Llandudno, 9 October 1948

The question is asked: What will happen when they [the Soviets] get the atomic bomb themselves and have accumulated a large store? You can judge yourselves what will happen then by what is happening now ... If they can continue month after month disturbing and tormenting the world, trusting to our Christian and altruistic inhibitions against using this strange new power against them, what will they do when they themselves have large quantities of atomic bombs? What do you suppose would be the position this afternoon if it had been Communist Russia instead of Free Enterprise America which had created the atomic weapon? Instead of being a sombre guarantee of peace and freedom it would have become an irresistible method of human enslavement. No one in his senses can believe that we have a limitless period of time before us. We ought to bring matters to a head and make a final settlement. We ought not to go jogging along improvident, incompetent, waiting for something to turn up, by which I mean waiting for something bad for us to turn up. The Western Nations will be far more likely to reach a lasting settlement, without bloodshed, if they formulate their just demands while they have the atomic power and before the Russian Communists have got it too.

Source J: party political broadcast given by Churchill on 8 October 1951

But rearmament is only half a policy. Unless you are armed and strong you cannot expect any mercy from the Communists; but if you are armed and strong you make a bargain with them which might rid the world of the terror in which it now lies and relieve us all from much of the impoverishment and privations into which we shall otherwise certainly sink.

The Conservative and Liberal Parties and part of the Socialist Party support the policy of rearmament and the effective binding together of all the nations all over the world outside the Iron Curtain, not because we are seeking war, but because we believe it is the only method by which a reasonable and lasting settlement might be reached. I believe that if the British Empire and Commonwealth joined together in fraternal association with the United States, and the growing power of Western Europe – including a reconciled France and Germany – worked together steadfastly, then the time will come, and may come sooner than is now expected, when a settlement may be reached which will give us peace for a long time. That is our heart's desire.

I do not hold that we should rearm in order to fight. I hold that we should rearm in order to parley [talk]. I hope and believe that there may be a parley. You will remember how, at Edinburgh in the 1950 election, I said that there should be a meeting with Soviet Russia, not of subordinates but of heads of governments in order to enable us at least to live peacefully together. You will remember, also, that this gesture, which I did not make without some knowledge of the personalities and forces involved, was curtly dismissed as an electioneering stunt. It might be that if such a meeting as I urged had taken place at that time the violent dangers of the Korean War and all that might spring out of it would not have come upon us.

Questions

1. Comment on Churchill's use of the word 'fraternal' in Source G. (3)
2. From Sources F and H, identify the threats to peace that concerned Churchill. (5)
3. Using Sources F, H and I, identify the 'just demands' that Churchill believed the West should make of the Soviet Union. (5)
4. In Sources I and J, Churchill focused on the threat of nuclear weapons to peace. With reference to both Sources and to your own knowledge, identify the differences in tone between the two speeches, and offer an explanation for these differences. (5)
5. With reference to all the Sources and to your own knowledge, comment on the view that Churchill's foreign policy outlook remained consistent in the years 1945 to 1955. (12)

Worked answer

2. In Source F Churchill first described the consequences of the Soviet takeover of Eastern and Central Europe, and the creation of 'Police governments' there, as dividing Europe into two spheres, with the 'iron curtain' as the demarcation and barrier between them. He particularly identifies the communist expansion as threatening Germany, divided into the four separate occupation zones and in an unstable state. In Source H he describes the physical and economic devastation of continental Europe as making the people there vulnerable to 'some new peril, tyranny or terror'. Source F particularly identifies the Soviet zone of Germany as being vulnerable to the imposition of a Soviet regime, leading to the destabilisation of the whole Central European region, and perhaps recreating the instability that contributed to the outbreak of the two world wars. In Source H Churchill stated that 'Germany must be deprived of the power to rearm', and in Source F that Europe work to ensure that Germany not be able to exploit the rivalry between the West and the Soviets to its advantage. In Source H he makes it clear that without a reconciliation between Germany and France, Europe would not be strong enough to withstand the expansionism of the Soviets.

NOTES

1. RADICAL, 1900–1911

1. W. S. Churchill: *Thoughts and Adventures* (London 1932), pp. 5–6.
2. Quoted in P. Addison: *Churchill on the Home Front 1900–1955* (London 1992), p. 175.
3. R. Shannon: *The Crisis of Imperialism* (London 1976), p. 387.
4. J. Charmley: *Churchill: The End of Glory* (London 1993), p. 42.
5. Quoted in H. Pelling: 'Churchill and the Labour Movement', in R. Blake and W. Roger Louis (eds): *Churchill* (Oxford 1996), p. 115.
6. P. Addison: *Churchill on the Home Front*, p. 111.
7. P. Addison: 'Churchill and Social Reform', in R. Blake and W. Roger Louis: *Churchill*, p. 63.
8. V. Bonham Carter: *Winston Churchill as I Knew Him* (London 1965), p. 197.
9. N. Rose: *Churchill: An Unruly Life* (London 1994), p. 79.
10. J. Charmley: *Churchill: The End of Glory*, p. 37.
11. H. Pelling: 'Churchill and the Labour Movement', p. 116.
12. P. Addison: *Churchill on the Home Front*, p. 11.
13. W. S. Churchill's speech at Coatsbridge 1904: quoted in P. Addison: *Churchill on the Home Front*, p. 46.
14. P. Addison: *Churchill on the Home Front*, p. 3.
15. W. S. Churchill to W. Royle, 5/9/1911: quoted in P. Addison: *Churchill on the Home Front*, p. 150.
16. J. Charmley: *Churchill: The End of Glory*, p. 67.
17. P. Addison: *Churchill on the Home Front*, p. 136.
18. W. S. Churchill: *Thoughts and Adventures*, p. 44.
19. J. Charmley: *Churchill: The End of Glory*, p. 67.
20. V. Bonham Carter: *Churchill as I Knew Him*, p. 223.
21. *The Times*, 16 August 1911: quoted in P. Addison: *Churchill on the Home Front*, pp. 149–150.

22. N. Rose: *Churchill: An Unruly Life*, p. 78.
23. P. Addison: *Churchill on the Home Front*, p. 149.
24. K. Robbins: *Churchill* (London 1992) p. 48.
25. N. Rose: *Churchill: An Unruly Life*, p. 79.
26. P. Addison: *Churchill on the Home Front*, p. 129.
27. P. Addison: *Churchill on the Home Front*, p. 114.
28. W. S. Churchill, 15 July 1910: quoted in P. Addison: *Churchill on the Home Front*, p. 124.
Source A: W. S. Churchill: *Thoughts and Adventures* (London 1932). pp. 44–45.
Source B: Letter to *The Times*, 6 January 1911.
Source C: Letter to *The Times*, 6 January 1911.
Source D: Letter to *The Times*, 10 January 1911.
Source E: V. Bonham Carter: *Winston Churchill as I Knew Him* (London 1965), pp. 196–197.
Source F: J. Charmley: *Churchill: The End of Glory* (London 1993), pp. 64–65.
Source G: P. Addison: *Churchill on the Home Front 1900–1955* (London 1992), pp. 110–111.
Source H: *The Times* Editorial, 9 November 1910.
Source I: *The Times* Editorial, 21 November 1910.

2. WARMONGER, 1911–1915

1. W. S. Churchill: *The World Crisis* (London 1923), p. 44.
2. R. Blake: *Winston Churchill* (Oxford 1998), p. 44.
3. N. Rose: *Churchill: An Unruly Life* (London 1994), p. 124.
4. W. S. Churchill: *The World Crisis*, p. 121.
5. First Report of the Dardanelles Commission, 1917, p. 12.
6. W. S. Churchill: *The World Crisis*, pp. 172 and 188.
7. N. Rose: *Churchill: An Unruly Life*, p. 124.
8. First Report of the Dardanelles Commission, 1917, p. 21.
9. A. J. P. Taylor: *English History 1914–1945* (Oxford 1965), p. 50.
10. P. Neville: *Winston Churchill: Statesman or Opportunist?* (London 1996), p. 35.
11. W. S. Churchill: *The World Crisis*, Vol. V, p. 257.
12. N. Rose: *Churchill: An Unruly Life*, p. 76.
13. W. S. Churchill: *The World Crisis*, Vol. III, p. 256.
14. W. S. Churchill: *The World Crisis*, Vol. III, p. 256.
15. W. S. Churchill: *The World Crisis*, Vol. III, p. 239.
16. R. Blake: *Winston Churchill*, p. 22.
17. Letter of 12 August 1928 to Irwin (later Lord Halifax): quoted in R. Jenkins: *The Chancellors* (London 1998), p. 326.
18. R. Jenkins: *The Chancellors*, p. 311.

19. P. Addison: 'Churchill and Social Reform', in R. Blake and W. Roger Louis (eds): *Churchill* (Oxford 1996), p. 73.
20. A. J. P. Taylor: *English History*, p. 723.
21. V. Bonham Carter: *Winston Churchill as I Knew Him* (London 1965), p. 163.
Source A: Tim Coates (ed.): *Lord Kitchener and Winston Churchill: The Dardanelles Part I 1914–15* (London 2000), pp. 104–105.
Source B: W. S. Churchill: *The World Crisis* (London 1923). pp. 10–11.
Source C: W. S. Churchill: *The World Crisis*, pp. 165–166.
Source D: R. O'Neill: The Gallipoli Memorial Lecture: 'For Want of Criticism: The Tragedy of Gallipoli', 26 April 1990, Holy Trinity Church, London.
Source E: R. Rhodes James: *Gallipoli* (London 1999). p. 31.
Source F: J. Charmley: *Churchill: The End of Glory* (London 1993), pp. 51–52.
Source G: V. Bonham Carter: *Winston Churchill as I Knew Him* (London 1965), pp. 162–163.
Source H: N. Rose: *Churchill: An Unruly Life* (London 1994), p. 136.
Source I: J. Lukacs: *The Duel: Hitler vs. Churchill 10 May–31 July 1940* (London 2000), pp. 109–110 and 125.
Source J: J. Grigg: *Lloyd George: The People's Champion 1902–1911* (London 1997), pp. 66–77.

3. CHANCELLOR, 1924–1929

1. T. F. Lindsay and M. Harrington: *The Conservative Party 1918–1979* (London 1979), p. 71.
2. R. Jenkins: *The Chancellors* (London 1998), p. 310.
3. Lord Moran: *Winston Churchill: The Struggle for Survival, 1940–1965* (London 1966), p. 303.
4. R. Jenkins: *The Chancellors*, p. 320.
5. P. Addison: *Churchill on the Home Front 1900–1955* (London 1992), p. 236.
6. P. Addison: *Churchill on the Home Front 1900–1955*, p. 236.
7. N. Rose: *Churchill: An Unruly Life* (London 1994), p. 173.
8. P. Addison: *Churchill on the Home Front 1900–1955*, p. 236.
9. D. Carlton: *Churchill and the Soviet Union* (Manchester 2000), p. 36.
10. R. Jenkins: *The Chancellors*, pp. 317–318
11. P. Addison: *Churchill on the Home Front 1900–1955*, p. 262.
12. N. Rose: *Churchill: An Unruly Life*, p. 178.
13. D. Carlton: *Churchill and the Soviet Union*, p. 36.
14. N. Rose: *Churchill: An Unruly Life*, p. 177.

15. D. Carlton: *Churchill and the Soviet Union*, p. 35.
16. D. Carlton: *Churchill and the Soviet Union*, p. 35.
17. P. Addison: *Churchill on the Home Front 1900–1955*, p. 263.
18. R. Jenkins: *The Chancellors*, p. 321.
19. P. Addison: *Churchill on the Home Front 1900–1955*, p. 231.
Source A: J. M. Keynes: *The Economic Consequences of Mr Churchill* (London 1925), pp. 5–6.
Source B: C. Cross: *Philip Snowden* (London 1966), p. 218.
Source C: Letter to *The Times*, 3 February 1926.
Source D: R. Jenkins: *The Chancellors* (London 1998), pp. 309–310.
Source E: W. K. Haselden: 'The Budget and the Taxpayer'. *Daily Mirror*, 24 April 1928.
Source F: D. Low: 'Winston's Persuasive Eloquence, *Evening Standard*, 23 February 1929.
Source G: E. Shinwell in Charles Eade (ed.): *Churchill by His Contemporaries* (London 1953), pp. 75–76.
Source H: D. Carlton: *Churchill and the Soviet Union* (Manchester 2000), p. 36.
Source I: P. Addison: *Churchill on the Home Front 1900–1955* (London 1992), pp. 262–265.
Source J: N. Rose: *Churchill: An Unruly Life* (London 1994), pp. 175–176.

4. EXILE, 1929–1939

1. R. Blake: *Winston Churchill* (Oxford 1998), p. 60.
2. G. Stewart: *Burying Caesar. Churchill, Chamberlain and the Battle for the Tory Party* (London 1999), p. 97.
3. G. Stewart: *Burying Caesar: Churchill, Chamberlain and the Battle for the Tory Party*, p. 113.
4. P. Addison: *Churchill on the Home Front 1900–1955* (London 1992), p. 235.
5. P. Ziegler: 'Churchill and the Monarchy', in R. Blake and W. Roger Louis: *Churchill* (Oxford 1996), p. 193.
6. W. S. Churchill: *The Second World War. 1. The Gathering Storm* (London 1948), p. 188.
7. P. Addison: *Churchill on the Home Front 1900–1955*, p. 323.
8. D. C. Watt: 'Churchill and Appeasement', in R. Blake and W. Roger Louis, p. 214.
9. P. Addison: *Churchill on the Home Front 1900–1955*, p. 323.
10. W. S. Churchill: *My Early Life* (London 1930), p. 102.
11. K. Robbins: *Churchill* (London and New York 1992), p. 105.
12. Lord Cranborne: speech of 24 May 1867, quoted in S. C. Smith: *British Imperialism 1750–1970* (Cambridge 1998), p. 58.

13. N. Rose: *Churchill: An Unruly Life* (London 1994), p. 189.
14. W. S. Churchill: *The Second World War. 1. The Gathering Storm*, p. 71.
15. W. S. Churchill: *The Second World War. 1. The Gathering Storm*, p. 45.
16. N. Rose: *Churchill: An Unruly Life*, p. 189.
17. P. Addison: *Churchill on the Home Front 1900–1955*, p. 315.
18. P. Clarke: 'Churchill's Economic Ideas 1900–1930', in R. Blake and W. Roger Louis, p. 95.
19. P. Addison: *Churchill on the Home Front 1900–1955*, p. 311.
20. S. Gopal: 'Churchill and India', in R. Blake and W. Roger Louis, p. 459.
21. G. Stewart: *Burying Caesar. Churchill, Chamberlain and the Battle for the Tory Party*, p. 165.
22 P. Addison: *Churchill on the Home Front 1900–1955*, p. 302.
Source A: R. Blake: *Winston Churchill* (Oxford 1998), pp. 59–60.
Source B: G. Stewart: *Burying Caesar: Churchill, Chamberlain and the Battle for the Conservative Party* (London 1999), pp. 96–97.
Source C: P. Addison: *Churchill on the Home Front 1900–1955* (London pp. 314–315.
Source D: S. Strube: 'Old Indian Die-hard', *Daily Express*, 22 November 1935.
Source E: 'Nazi Movement – Local Version', *Daily Herald*, 30 March 1933.
Source F: W. S. Churchill: *The Second World War. 1. The Gathering Storm* (London 1948), p. 271.
Source G: A. Hitler: Speech of 9 October 1938 in Charles Eade (ed.): *Churchill by His Contemporaries* (London 1953). p. 139.
Source H: 'A Family Visit', *Punch*, 2 November 1938.
Source I: E. Shinwell in Charles Eade (ed.): *Churchill by His Contemporaries*, pp. 77–78.
Source J: P. Addison: *Churchill on the Home Front 1900–1955*, pp. 323–325.

5. FINEST HOUR

1. P. Hennessy: *Never Again: Britain 1945–1951* (London 1993), p. 17.
2. N. Rose: *Churchill: An Unruly Life* (London 1994), p. 261.
3. P. Hennessy: *Never Again: Britain 1945–1951*, p. 17.
4. S. S. Wilson: *The Cabinet Office to 1945* (London 1975), p. 93.
5. P. Addison: *The Road to 1945: British Politics and the Second World War* (London 1994), p. 65.

6. G. Stewart: *Burying Caesar: Churchill, Chamberlain and the Battle for the Tory Party* (London 1999), p. 392.
7. P. Addison: *The Road to 1945: British Politics and the Second World War*, p. 81.
8. P. Addison: *The Road to 1945: British Politics and the Second World War*, p. 61.
9. T. Corfield: 'Why Chamberlain Really Fell' in *History Today* (December 1996), p. 25.
10. P. Addison: *The Road to 1945: British Politics and the Second World War*, p. 58.
11. P. Addison: *The Road to 1945: British Politics and the Second World War*, p. 92.
12. W. S. Churchill: *The Second World War. 1. The Gathering Storm* (London 1948), p. 532.
13. D. Reynolds: 'Churchill in 1940: The Worst and Finest Hour', in R. Blake and W. Roger Louis (eds) *Churchill* (Oxford 1996), p. 249.
14. Quoted in J. Lukacs: *Five Days in London, May 1940* (New Haven and London 1999), p. 118.
15. G. Stewart: *Burying Caesar: Churchill, Chamberlain and the Battle for the Tory Party*, p. 430.
16. R. Overy: *Why the Allies Won* (London 1995), p. 266.
17. W. S. Churchill: speech of 17 June 1940.
18. H. Dalton: diary entry for 28 May 1940, quoted in G. Stewart: *Burying Caesar: Churchill, Chamberlain and the Battle for the Tory Party*, p. 433.
19. G. Stewart: *Burying Caesar: Churchill, Chamberlain and the Battle for the Tory Party*, p. 433.
20. J. Charmley: *Churchill: The End of Glory* (London 1993), pp. 405–407.
21. W. S. Churchill: *The Second World War. 2. Their Finest Hour* (London 1949), p. 266.
22. R. Lamb: *Churchill as War Leader: Right or Wrong?* (London 1991), p. 52.
23. J. Lukacs: *Five Days in London, May 1940*, p. 217.
Source A: R. Boothby: letter to Churchill. 9 May 1940 in *Churchill: The War Leader* (document pack produced by Imperial War Museum, Public Record Office and Churchill College, c. 1998).
Source B: P. Addison: *Churchill on the Home Front 1900–1955* (London 1992). pp. 329–330.
Source C: W. S. Churchill: *The Second World War. 1. The Gathering Storm* (London 1948), pp. 528–529.
Source D: G. Stewart: *Burying Caesar: Churchill, Chamberlain and the Battle for the Conservative Party* (London 1999), pp. 416–417.

Source E: J. Colville in J. Wheeler Bennett (ed.): *Action This Day* (London 1968), p. 48.

Source F: Lord Ismay: *The Memoirs of Lord Ismay* (London 1960), pp. 146–147.

Source G: J. Charmley: *Churchill: The End of Glory* (London 1993), p. 403.

Source H: B. Pimlott (ed.): *The Second World War Diary of Hugh Dalton* (London 1986), pp. 27–28.

Source I: W. S. Churchill: *The Second World War. 2. Their Finest Hour* (London 1949), p. 114.

Source J: J. Lukacs: *Five Days in London May 1940* (New Haven and London 1999), pp. 188–189.

6. WARLORD, 1940–1945

1. Quoted in R. Overy: *Why the Allies Won* (London 1995), p. 270.
2. Lord Justice Birkett: 'Churchill the Orator', in Charles Eade (ed.): *Churchill, by his Contemporaries* (London 1953), p. 225.
3. Ed Murrow quoted in D. J. Wenden: 'Churchill, Radio and Cinema', in R. Blake and W. Roger Louis (eds): *Churchill* (Oxford 1996), p.222.
4. D. Jablonsky: *Churchill, the Great Game and Total War* (1991), p. 123.
5. W. S. Churchill: 'Be Ye Men of Valour' speech of 19 May 1940.
6. W. S. Churchill: speech of 20 August 1940.
7. W. S. Churchill: 'We shall fight on the beaches' speech of 4 June 1940.
8. John Colville: *The Fringes of Power: Downing Street Diaries 1939–1955* (London 1985), p. 217.
9. W. S. Churchill: *The Second World War. 1. The Gathering Storm* (London 1948), p. 253.
10. W. S. Churchill: speech of 13 May 1940.
11. W. S. Churchill: speech of 4 June 1940.
12. D. J. Wenden: 'Churchill, Radio and Cinema', p. 224.
13. D. J. Wenden: 'Churchill, Radio and Cinema', p. 236.
14. P. Addison: *Churchill on the Home Front 1900–1955* (London 1992), p. 336.
15. P. Addison: *Churchill on the Home Front 1900–1955*, p. 335.
16. P. Addison: *Churchill on the Home Front 1900–1955*, p. 335.
17. P. Addison: *Churchill on the Home Front 1900–1955*, p. 337.
18. P. Addison: *Churchill on the Home Front 1900–1955*, p. 337.
19. R. Overy: *Why the Allies Won*, p. 264.
20. J. Charmley: *Churchill: The End of Glory* (London 1993), p. 493.
21. D. Carlton: *Churchill and the Soviet Union* (Manchester 2000), p. 98.

22. J. Keegan: 'Churchill's Strategy', in R. Blake and W. Roger Louis, p. 350.
23. D. Carlton: *Churchill and the Soviet Union*, p. 115.
24. D. Judd: *Empire: The British Imperial Experience, from 1765 to the Present* (London 1997), p. 317.
25. N. Rose: *Churchill: An Unruly Life* (London 1994), p. 310.
26. N. Rose: *Churchill: An Unruly Life*, p. 303.
27. Peter Dewey: *War and Progress: Britain 1914–1945* (1997), p. 296.
28. J. Charmley: *Churchill: The End of Glory*, p. 455.
29. J. Lukacs: *The Duel: Hitler vs. Churchill 10 May–31 July 1940* (London 2000), p. 232.
30. R. Overy: *Why the Allies Won*, p. 246.
Source A: Churchill on the steps of Number 10 Downing St, 10 May 1940, IWM HU 53578.
Source B: Lord Ismay: *The Memoirs of Lord Ismay* (London 1960), pp 179–180.
Source C: Last page of Churchill's speech of 18 June 1940, CHAR 9/140/55.
Source D: D. J. Wenden: 'Churchill and the Cinema' in R. Blake and W. Roger Louis (eds): *Churchill: A Major New Assessment of His Life in Peace and War* (Oxford 1996), p. 221.
Source E: The Prime Minister on tour, IWM H 14266.
Source F: The Prime Minister in Cherbourg, IWM OWIL 30645.
Source G: 'Let Us Go Forward Together' Ministry of Information poster, IWM MH 6790.
Source H: W. S. Churchill: speech of 22 June 1941.
Source I: W. S. Churchill: speech of 24 August 1941.
Source J: J. Colville: *The Fringes of Power: Downing Street Diaries 1939–1955* (London 1985), pp. 562–564.
Source K: J. Charmley: *Churchill: The End of Glory* (London 1993), p. 455.

7. CONTROVERSIES

1. W. S. Churchill: speech of 24 August 1941, quoted in R. Breitman: *Official Secrets: What the Nazis Planned and What the British and Americans Knew* (London 2000), p. 93.
2. W. S. Churchill to Eden, 11 July 1944, quoted in W. S. Churchill: *The Second World War. 6. Triumph and Tragedy* (London 1954), p. 549.
3. Sinclair to Eden, 15 July 1944, quoted in M. Gilbert: *Auschwitz and the Allies* (New York 1981), p. 285.
4. Cavendish-Bentinck note, 17 July 1943, quoted in M. Gilbert: *Auschwitz and the Allies*, p. 150.

5. C. Portal memo, 2 January 1943, quoted in M. Gilbert: *Auschwitz and the Allies*, p. 106.
6. A. Eden: speech to the House of Commons, 25 February 1943.
7. R. Breitman: *Official Secrets: What the Nazis Planned and What the British and Americans Knew*, p. 105.
8. R. Breitman: *Official Secrets: What the Nazis Planned and What the British and Americans Knew*, p. 228.
9. Max Hastings: *Bomber Command* (London 1999), p. 342.
10. Max Hastings: *Bomber Command*, p. 342.
11. N. Davies: *Europe: A History* (Oxford 1996), p. 415.
12. N. Rose: *Churchill: An Unruly Life* (London 1994), p. 274.
13. W. S. Churchill at Cabinet, 3 September 1940: PRO CAB 66/11, WP(40)352.
14. R. Overy: *Why the Allies Won* (London 1995), p. 103.
15. B. Bond: *War and Society in Europe, 1870–1970* (London 1984), p. 152.
16. W. S. Churchill quoted in M. Carver: 'Churchill and the Defence Chiefs', in R. Blake and W. Roger Louis (eds): *Churchill* (Oxford 1996), p. 368.
17. M. Hastings: *Bomber Command*, p. 12.
18. M. Hastings: *Bomber Command*, p. 341.
19. M. Hastings: *Bomber Command*, p. 341.
20. W. S. Churchill minute to Chiefs of Staff, 28 March 1945: PRO CAB 120/303.
21. M. Hastings: *Bomber Command*, p. 344.
22. M. Hastings: *Bomber Command*, p. 133.
23. M. Hastings: *Bomber Command*, p. 301.
24. J. Keegan: *The Second World War* (London 1989), p. 361.
25. Quoted in N. Rose: *Churchill: An Unruly Life* pp. 274–275.
Source A: Letter from Anthony Eden to Archibald Sinclair, 7 July 1944 from the Holocaust Exhibition, Imperial War Museum (2000).
Source B: Minute from Sinclair to Eden, 15 July 1944 from the Holocaust Exhibition, Imperial War Museum (2000).
Source C: Minute from Air Commodore Grant to Cavendish-Bentinck, 13 August 1944 from the Holocaust Exhibition, Imperial War Museum (2000).
Source D: Text from the Holocaust Exhibition, Imperial War Museum (2000).
Source E: Information taken from Martin Gilbert: *Auschwitz and the Allies* (New York 1981), *passim*.
Source F: Bomber Command briefing on Dresden: reprinted in Max Hastings: *Bomber Command* (London 1999), p. 342.
Source G: M. Gilbert: *Churchill: A Life* (London 1993), p. 567.
Source H: M. Hastings: *Bomber Command*, p. 341.
Source I: Memo from Churchill to the Chiefs of Staff, 28 March 1945, CAB 120/303.

Source J: Memo from Churchill to the Chiefs of Staff, 1 April 1945, published in M. Hastings: *Bomber Command*, p. 344.

8. ELDER, 1945–1955

1. W. S. Churchill: statement of resignation, 26 July 1945, CHAR 20/195A/79.
2. N. Rose: *Churchill: An Unruly Life* (London 1994), p. 334.
3. N. Rose: *Churchill: An Unruly Life*, p. 335.
4. N. Rose: *Churchill: An Unruly Life*, p. 335.
5. N. Rose: *Churchill: An Unruly Life*, p. 387.
6. P. Addison: *Churchill on the Home Front 1900–1955* (London 1992), p. 424.
7. P. Addison: *Churchill on the Home Front*, p. 413.
8. A. Sked and C. Cook: *Post-war Britain: A Political History* (Harmondsworth 1983), p. 103.
9. A. Sked and C. Cook: *Post-war Britain: A Political History*, p. 94.
10. A. Sked and C. Cook: *Post-war Britain: A Political History*, pp. 94–95.
11. A. Sked and C. Cook: *Post-war Britain: A Political History*, p. 112.
12. P. Hennessy: *The Prime Minister: The Office and its Holders since 1945* (London 2000), p. 205.
13. P. Addison: *Churchill on the Home Front*, p. 426.
14. P. Addison: *Churchill on the Home Front*, p. 420.
15. N. Rose: *Churchill: An Unruly Life*, p. 331.
16. W. S. Churchill: 'Sinews of Peace' speech, 5 March 1946: quoted in *The Sinews of Peace: Post-war Speeches by Winston S. Churchill*, edited by Randolph S. Churchill (London 1948), p. 103.
17. N. Rose: *Churchill: An Unruly Life*, p. 333.
18. W. S. Churchill: 'Sinews of Peace' speech, 5 March 1946, p. 101.
19. D. Carlton: *Churchill and the Soviet Union* (Manchester 2000), p. 142.
20. W. S. Churchill: 'Sinews of Peace' speech, 5 March 1946, p. 103.
21. W. S. Churchill: 'Sinews of Peace' speech, 5 March 1946, p. 103.
22. F. J. Harbutt: *The Iron Curtain: Churchill, America and the Origins of the Cold War* (Oxford and New York 1986), p. 281.
23. W. S. Churchill: 'Sinews of Peace' speech, 5 March 1946, p. 103.
24. W. S. Churchill 'Sinews of Peace' speech, 5 March 1946, p. 98.
25. J. Ramsden: 'Mr Churchill goes to Fulton', in J. W. Muller (ed.): *Churchill's Iron Curtain Speech Fifty Years on* (London 1999), p. 45.
26. H. Kissinger: *Diplomacy* (London 1994), p. 466.
27. H. Kissinger: *Diplomacy*, p. 466.
28. W. S. Churchill: speech at Llandudno, 9 October 1948: quoted in

Europe Unite: Speeches 1947 and 1948 by Winston S. Churchill, edited by Randolph S. Churchill (London 1950), pp. 412–414.

29. W. S. Churchill: speech at Zurich University, 19 September 1946: quoted in *The Sinews of Peace: Post-War Speeches of Winston S. Churchill*, pp. 199–201.

30. M. Beloff: 'Churchill and Europe', in R. Blake and W. Roger Louis (eds): *Churchill* (Oxford 1996), p. 446.

31. M. Beloff: 'Churchill in Europe', p. 453.

32. W. S. Churchill: speech at Zurich University, 19 September 1946: quoted in *The Sinews of Peace: Post-War Speeches of Winston S. Churchill*, edited by Randolph S. Churchill (London 1948), p. 199.

33. W. S. Churchill: party political broadcast, 8 October 1951: quoted in *Stemming the Tide: The Speeches 1951 and 1952 by Winston S. Churchill* (London 1953), p. 135.

34. H. Kissinger: *Diplomacy*, p. 508.

35. D. Carlton: *Churchill and the Soviet Union*, p. 178.

36. D. Carlton: *Churchill and the Soviet Union*, p. 170.

37. D. Carlton: *Churchill and the Soviet Union*, p. 162.

Source A: T. E. Lindsay and M. Harrington: *The Conservative Party 1918–1979* (London 1974), p. 173.

Source B: J. Colville: *The Fringes of Power: Downing Street Diaries 1939–1955* (London 1985), pp. 654–707.

Source C: Lord Normanbrook in J. Wheeler Bennett (ed.): *Action This Day* (London 1968), pp. 37–44.

Source D: Lord Moran: *Winston Churchill: The Struggle for Survival 1940–1965* (London 1966), p. 614.

Source E: R. Jenkins: *Churchill* (New York 2001), p. 897.

Source F: W. S. Churchill: speech, 5 March 1946 in *The Sinews of Peace: Post-War Speeches by Winston S. Churchill*, edited by Randolph S. Churchill (London 1948), pp. 100–101.

Source G: W. S. Churchill: speech, 5 March 1946 in *The Sinews of Peace: Post-War Speeches by Winston S. Churchill*, p. 98.

Source H: W. S. Churchill: speech, 19 September 1946 in *The Sinews of Peace: Post-War Speeches by Winston S. Churchill*, p. 310.

Source I: W. S. Churchill: speech, 9 October 1948 in *Europe Unite: Speeches 1947 and 1948 by Winston S. Churchill*, edited by Randolph S. Churchill (London 1950), pp. 414–415.

Source J: W. S. Churchill: party political broadcast, 8 October 1951 in *Stemming the Tide: The Speeches 1951 and 1952 by Winston S. Churchill*, edited by Randolph S. Churchill (London 1953), pp. 134–135.

SELECT BIBLIOGRAPHY

PRIMARY SOURCES

Churchill wrote two key histories of this period, both running to several volumes. *The World Crisis* is in five volumes: Vol. I, 1911–1914; Vol. II, 1915; Vol. III, 1916–1918 Part I; Vol. IV, 1916–1918 Part II; and Vol. V: *The Aftermath* (London 1923–1929). *The Second World War* is in six volumes: Vol. I, *The Gathering Storm*; Vol. II, *Their Finest Hour*; Vol. III, *The Grand Alliance*; Vol. IV, *The Hinge of Fate*; Vol. V, *Closing the Ring*; and Vol. VI, *Triumph and Tragedy* (London 1948–1954). Both of these series have been condensed into smaller editions, which may be more accessible for students: *The World Crisis 1911–1918*, two volumes (London 1938), and *The Second World War* (Harmondsworth, reprinted 1989).

Churchill did not keep a diary, but a surprising number of the people who worked with him during the Second World War did. John Colville: *The Fringes of Power: Downing Street Diaries 1939–1955* (London 1985) is both an entertaining and informative read, by one of Churchill's favourite private secretaries. Alanbrooke, Churchill's Chief of General Staff, also wrote a diary of the war years which has recently been re-edited by Alex Danchev and Daniel Todman: *War Diaries 1939–1945: Field Marshal Lord Alanbrooke* (London 2001).

Other useful sources include memoirs and recollections of people close to Churchill. Violet Bonham Carter: *Winston Churchill as I Knew Him* (London 1965) recalls Churchill's years as a young Liberal politician. Lord Ismay: *The Memoirs of Lord Ismay* (London 1960) and Sir John Wheeler-Bennett: *Action This Day: Working with Churchill* (London 1968) are both useful sources for the 1930s and the war years. The original Dardanelles Report has been published in full as *Lord Kitchener and Winston Churchill: The Dardanelles Part I 1914–15* by the Stationery Office (London 2000).

SECONDARY SOURCES

There is a large number of biographies of Churchill and so what follows is a selection of those that are the most accessible for students of AS and A2. Martin Gilbert is Churchill's official biographer. The full biography runs to several large volumes but a single-volume edition is available: Martin Gilbert: *Churchill: A Life* (London 1993). Short and pithy biographies include Keith Robbins: *Churchill* (London and New York 1992) and Robert Blake: *Winston Churchill* (Oxford 1998). Of the longer biographies, one of the most readable is Norman Rose: *Churchill: An Unruly Life* (London 1994). For more polemical views of Churchill's career: John Charmley: *Churchill: The End of Glory* (London 1993) and David Carlton: *Churchill and the Soviet Union* (Manchester 2000). A very useful collection of essays on a wide range of topics is edited by Robert Blake and W. Roger Louis: *Churchill: A Major New Assessment of His Life in Peace and War* (Oxford 1996). For Churchill's domestic politics, Paul Addison: *Churchill on the Home Front 1900–1955* (London 1992) is an excellent account, as is his account of the wartime coalition government, *The Road to 1945* (London 1994). The period from 1929 to the outbreak of the Second World War is the focus of Graham Stewart in *Burying Caesar: Churchill, Chamberlain and the Battle for the Tory Party* (London 1999). His post-war government is dealt with in Peter Hennessy: *The Prime Minister: The Office and its Holders since 1945* (London 2000) and Chris Cook and Alan Sked: *Postwar Britain* (second edition London 1984).

WEBSITES

www.winstonchurchill.org is a comprehensive website maintained by the Churchill Center in Washington, DC. It includes reviews of and debates about books on Churchill's life, facts, myths and frequently asked questions, and his complete speeches.

www.churchill.nls.ac.uk is a useful resource based on documentary evidence provided by the Churchill Archive and written by the National Library of Scotland. This includes activities created for students studying for Scottish Highers.

FURTHER SOURCES

Blenheim Palace, the ancestral home of Churchill's family, near Bladon in Oxfordshire. Call 01993 811 091 for details of opening times and the education service or see www.blenheim palace.org.

Cabinet War Rooms, the Whitehall underground complex in which Churchill and his government lived and worked for much of the Second World War. A Churchill Museum is planned to open there in 2005. Call 020 7747 8332 for details of the education service or see www.iwm.org.uk

Chartwell, Churchill's family home in Westerham, Kent, now managed by the National Trust. Call 01732 868 381 for details of opening times.

Churchill Archives Centre, based at Churchill College, Cambridge. Call 01223 336 087 for information about access to the documents held there or see www.chu.cam.ac.uk/ archives/home.shtml.

INDEX

Phoney War 69, 74
Poland 94, 128; Poles 108–9; *see also* Warsaw Uprising
Potsdam conference; *see* wartime conferences
prisoners of war 108, 116
prison reform 3
protectionism; *see* tariff reform

rationing 90, 91, 124
Roosevelt, Franklin 90, 92, 93–4, 103; *see also* USA
Russian Civil War 34; *see also* Bolsheviks; Soviets

Second World War 24–5, 26, 42, 56
shell supply crisis 22
siege of Sidney Street 7, 11–12
Simon Commission 57; *see also* India
'Sinews of Peace' speech 136, 137; *see also* iron curtain
Singapore, fall of 90
social reform 4–5, 38; *see also* Coal Mines Act; Old Age Pensions Act; People's Budget, Trades Board Act
South Africa 2, 3
Soviet Union; *see* USSR
Soviets 48, 119, 127, 128; *see also* Russian Civil War
Stalin, Jozef 87, 89, 90, 93–4,138; 'naughty' document 94; Moscow meeting 112; *see also* USSR
strikes of 1911; *see* industrial unrest
Suez 94, 104
Suffragettes 7, 9, 15

tariff reform 1, 3, 37, 51; *see also* free trade
taxation 38
Teheran conference; *see* wartime conferences
Ten Year Rule 34

Tonypandy 7, 39, 41, 106
Trade Boards Act 1909 4
trade unions 8, 9, 39, 41, 46–9
Truman, Harry 126, 128, 130–1
TUC 49

USA 77, 84, 87, 92, 94, 95, 112, 122; wartime relations 92–7, 104; postwar relations 127–8, 131–3, 138; *see also* lend-lease; Roosevelt; Truman
USSR 42, 84, 87, 92, 94, 96, 111, 128, 130; second front 93; deportation of Hungarian Jews 107–9; wartime relations 92–7, 104; postwar relations 127–8, 131–3, 138; *see also* Stalin
unconditional surrender 95
'united states of Europe' speech, 131; *see also* Europe

Wall Street Crash 52
War Cabinet; *see* Cabinet
War Council; *see* Cabinet
Warsaw Uprising 109, 116, 118; *see also* Poles; Poland
Wartime conferences, Potsdam 128; Teheran 128; Yalta 112–13, 120, 128
Widows and Old Age Pensions Act 1925 38
Wood, Sir Kingsley 72
World War One *see* First World War
World War Two see Second World War

Yalta conference *see* wartime conferences

Zinoviev letter 35, 41, 53
Zurich speech 131, 137; *see also* Europe